James E. Vincent

THE BASIS OF CRITICISM IN THE ARTS

The Basis of Criticism In the Arts

BY

STEPHEN C. PEPPER

*Professor of Philosophy and Aesthetics
in the University of California*

Cambridge, Massachusetts
HARVARD UNIVERSITY PRESS
1956

To my
FATHER AND MOTHER

Preface

THESE LECTURES have grown into their present shape by a process of accretion. In the summer of 1944 I was asked to give at Harvard a series of three lectures on Aesthetics and for that purpose planned the lectures on the four types of criticism, intending to read three of them as samples of what I conceived to be sound critical procedure. But I soon discovered that a whole lecture would be needed to explain the method I was advocating and the reasons why I thought this method necessary. Thus a lecture on the method became the first one of the series delivered at Harvard and was followed by the two on Mechanism and Contextualism.

The lecture on method when delivered proved to be a source for still further questions about the philosophy that lay behind it. These comments indicated an Introduction. Other comments as to how the method of criticism proposed would work out in actual practice led to the last lecture.

The addition of the Supplementary Essay is almost self-explanatory. Though I had worked out in detail the analysis of the aesthetic work of art given in this essay, it could not without disproportion be introduced into the actual lecture series. Yet the brief reference to this analysis in the third lecture seemed inadequate, in view of publication, particularly since the work of art was the object on which the whole series was focused. So, I solved the problem by simply adding the analysis as a supplement.

The whole series except the last lecture was delivered in the fall of 1944 at the University of California, Berkeley.

The lectures show internally a wide indebtedness, and besides they have profited from many critics in the audiences who heard them, as well as from numbers in Berkeley and elsewhere who have listened to the ideas before ever they were organized in writing. But above all I wish to express my gratitude to the Harvard Philosophy Department for the stimulus and the opportunity they gave to bring these ideas into their present form and to have them published, and for their hospitality in inviting me to give the lectures in Cambridge.

S. C. P.

Berkeley, California
August 1, 1945

Acknowledgments

THE AUTHOR is indebted to the following persons or publishers for permission to quote from copyright material: to Macmillan & Co., Ltd., for permission to quote from *Three Lectures on Aesthetic*, by Bernard Bosanquet; to Minton, Balch & Co., for *Art as Experience*, by John Dewey; to W. W. Norton & Co., for *Arts and the Man*, by Irwin Edman; to the Oxford University Press and the poet's family, for *Poems of Gerard Manley Hopkins*; to *The Journal of Philosophy*, for "Value and the Situation," by Otis Lee; to Mr. Peter Smith, for *The Craft of Fiction*, by Percy Lubbock; to Northwestern University Studies for *The Aesthetic Process*, by Bertram Morris; to Charles Scribner's Sons for *The Sense of Beauty*, by George Santayana.

Contents

THE BASIS OF CRITICISM IN THE ARTS

Introduction

THESE LECTURES on the basis of criticism in the arts are really a philosophy of criticism. There is a definite philosophy underlying them, but one so empirical in conception that anyone more interested in criticism than philosophy does not need to get deeply involved in it. He needs only to keep his eye on the relevant facts, and to see if the instruments of criticism are adequate to deal with them. All that the philosophy does is to see to it that all the relevant facts are brought into consideration. But I find that there are a good many people who would like to know more about this underlying philosophy than is brought out by the lectures. This knowledge can be obtained in a fully worked out form in *World Hypotheses*,[1] a philosophical study of evidence, fact, knowledge, and philosophy. The present lectures are one application, and also I hope a partial verification, of the principles there arrived at. But for the benefit of the philosophically interested reader who desires something between the full account of these principles and the bare minimum of reference to them contained in the coming lectures, I give here a brief summary of the contents of *World Hypotheses*.

As I said, that book is a study of evidence. It is a study of the sources, nature, and organization of evidence, and of the best hypotheses at present available as to what this evidence is about or as to how it is interrelated. Since the problem of

[1] Stephen C. Pepper, *World Hypotheses* (Berkeley and Los Angeles: University of California Press, 1942).

criticism is ultimately the problem of the evidence for the legitimacy of the criteria of criticism, the bearing of the broader study of evidence without restriction on the more restricted study of the evidences for justifiable criticism, is clear enough. I proceed, now, to the summary.

In *World Hypotheses* I first showed the illegitimacy of both utter skepticism and dogmatism in cognition. Utter skepticism, so far as it can be made intelligible at all, turns out to be a species of dogmatism. When a man declares, "Nothing exists," or "Nothing is known at all," he does not seem to be commit-ting himself to any cognitive responsibility. He seems to be playing safe and relieving himself of all demands for evidence. Actually, he is just as responsible as if he declared, "I know all things and their nature is such and such." He must produce evidence for his sweeping denial of the trustworthiness of evidence; otherwise, there is no reason to accept his declaration. The point is that anyone who wishes to establish a skeptical position can only seek to do so in the same way as anyone who expects more positive results, that is, by looking for the evidence and, if one is a skeptic, hoping to find it wanting, and, if one is not a skeptic, hoping to find it available. With either attitude, if one is honest, one is willing to follow the evidence wherever it points, whenever it appears. What the final results will be only the evidence can show. Skepticism in excess of the evidence, or without any evidence, is not canniness in knowledge but is dogmatic. The application of this general judgment of the skeptical attitude to the field of aesthetic criticism can well be taken to heart. For skeptics of criticism arise periodically in schools and are likely to be even more irresponsible in the production of evidence for their position than the positive dogmatists of criticism whom they delight in castigating.

The illegitimacy of dogmatism is plain from its definition. I define dogmatism as an attitude of belief (or disbelief) in excess of the grounds of belief (or disbelief). Where a balancing of evidence is admitted, the application of this definition rarely produces a serious problem. But there is a particular field of cognition that has been a breeding ground of dogmatism (not the appeal to infallible authority, which is seldom made today, though when it is made it is clearly dogmatic, since the statement of an authority is never good evidence in itself, but only because we trust that the authority has found sufficient other evidence to support it). The great breeding ground of dogmatism today is the appeal to certainty. Reasons were shown in *World Hypotheses* for questioning any belief proposed on the ground of its certainty without other evidential support. I questioned there the appeal to the self-evidence of any principles, and to the indubitability of any descriptions of fact. The appeal to certainty in all its manifestations, which are legion, was rejected. I was not denying that we may have access to many incorrigible or pure facts, and that we may today know some absolutely true principles, but I did deny that there was any other way of establishing such facts or principles except by noting the evidence that they were always confirmed. I showed reasons for maintaining that the only secure grounds for belief are through empirical evidence, and through the corroboration of such evidence.

This point is important to notice in aesthetic considerations, because nowhere is appeal so constantly made to intuitive certainty. Basic aesthetic facts are largely immediacies (such as feelings, emotions, sensations, intuited forms), and aesthetic writers are constantly presenting their descriptions of these immediacies as indubitable and then blandly drawing critical consequences as if they thought their feet were set upon the pillars of the firmament. This is simple dogmatism. Descriptions of immediacies require, if anything, more careful confirmation than more impersonal evidence. They are particularly subject to unnoticed interpretation. If you ask, Why not appeal to the immediacies themselves? the answer is that that is just what everybody thinks he is doing when he offers his descriptions. Unquestionably we all have our immediacies, but when we offer them as evidence we are always offering our descriptions of them, and we have no way of telling how accurate these descriptions are except by the corroboration of further evidence. In our coming study of criticism, therefore, we shall never appeal to the certainty of the immediately given, for experience has shown that to do so is dogmatic. We can never be certain of just what is immediately given. And as for appeals to the *a priori* certainty, or self-evidence of critical principles, that is already quite widely regarded as simple minded. Our study will be empirical throughout. Our results will consequently be probable only and never utterly conclusive. Nevertheless, we shall always be able to show the balance of evidence for our judgments, or, at least, be willing to acknowledge the legitimacy of a demand that we do so.

The grounds for belief are accordingly always in terms of weight of evidence, which means in terms of the amount of corroboration of evidence that can be achieved. After establishing this principle, I then called attention to two kinds of corroboration, which were called multiplicative and structural. Multiplicative corroboration gives us the kind of facts which we associate with physics and with the sciences generally. It is the corroboration that comes from taking an observation repeatedly (or as often as we think necessary) till we are quite sure there has been no error. It is the corroboration of one observation with another, or of one man with another, where the fact observed is supposed to be exactly identical in the different observations. It is that identical fact that is said to be corroborated. It is a corroboration of man by man. Facts so corroborated were called *data*. Experimental *data* in terms of measurements or pointer readings and correlations among pointer readings are the highest refinement of such data.

Structural corroboration is the corroboration of fact with fact. It is not a multiplicity of observations of one identical fact, but an observed convergence of many different facts towards one result. We have a crude use of it in what we call circumstantial evidence, where a variety of different circumstances all point to a single conclusion. Repetitions of observations are frequently impossible. Wherever a question arises over a past historical event, for instance, the observation of that event can never be repeated and corroboration has to be made in terms of a convergence of evidence in terms of other facts than the one in question towards the probability of the nature of that event. Such corroboration requires a hypothesis to indicate the way in which the evidence may converge to corroborate a fact. The hypothesis holds all the corroborating facts together in a system and, in so far as the hypothesis is verified, the whole system of facts gains in probability. That is, every new fact that is added to the system of evidence and fits in with the hypothesis tends to corroborate not only the central fact at issue but also all the other facts in the system in their relation to the hypothesis. Such facts as these established by structural corroboration were called *danda*.

The distinction between *data* and *danda* is important for our coming study because most aesthetic facts are *danda* rather than *data*. Attempts have been made to accumulate aesthetic data, aesthetic observations multiplicatively corroborated, and the pretty thin showing of experimental aesthetics from the psychological laboratories is the result. Aesthetic control by the artist of his materials is essentially of the structural type. He makes his poetic word, or his chord, or his linear shape more and more aesthetically precise by his arrangement of other words, and chords, and shapes in its context. The great laboratories of aesthetics are the workshops and studios of the artists and the facts that have come out of these are almost all danda. The data of aesthetics are mostly rather trivial. The overwhelming mass of aesthetic facts and nearly all its important facts are danda.

Consequently, attempts to make aesthetics and criticism narrowly scientific on the analogy of physics miss the characteristic nature of the subject. For progress in aesthetics and criticism one must look to structural corroboration and work deliberately in that field. That is our aim in the coming lectures.

Now, the cognitive strength of a structural hypothesis is in proportion to the scope and the precision of the corroborative material. For maximum cognitive strength we thus reach the conception of hypotheses of unrestricted scope and maximum precision. Only in such unrestricted hypotheses have we the security that there are no outlying facts which will fail to support the hypothesis and its system of structural corroboration. Such unrestricted systems of structural corroboration I call world hypotheses. They are often called philosophies.

In tracing the main evidential support of criticism to structural corroboration, and thence finding that we are thereby led to world hypotheses, we discover that criticism is philosophical in its foundations. Sound criticism is the application of a sound philosophy to works of art.

This has frequently been affirmed. We now see the reason for it. But this conclusion has also often been shunned for fear it committed criticism to something arbitrary, *a priori*, and unempirical. There has been some justification for this fear. Philosophy has been used by dogmatic critics of the past as a shelter for their dogmatisms. But the obvious comment about such fears is that a dogmatic philosophy is not a sound philosophy. A sound philosophy is an empirical one, nothing more than as complete a systematization of the world's evidence as can be made, nothing more than a world hypothesis describing the structural lines of corroboration of evidence. In applying world hypotheses to the problem of criticism we are simply making use of *all* the evidence available, so that our judgments may have the widest possible empirical base. And this is precisely what I wish to bring out in the coming lectures.

But in *World Hypotheses* it appeared that there are a number of alternative ways of organizing the world's evidence; that is, that there are a number of alternative world hypotheses. These are not so many as a glance through a history of philosophy would lead one to think. Different philosophers with different vocabularies and superficially different statements turn out to be handling evidence along the same structural lines, and so to be exponents of the same world hypothesis. Through the whole history of human thought there have probably been only about seven world hypotheses conceived in this broad sense, and of these seven, reasons were advanced in my book for regarding only four as worthy of serious consideration today. The evidence for the others is so much inferior to that for the four most adequate ones that these are the only ones from which we can expect reliable assistance in reaching sound judgments.

These four I called formism, mechanism, contextualism, and organicism. None is completely corroborated by its evidence, so that we cannot accept any of them as an entirely true or adequate description of our world. We might regard them as four different approximations to the nature of the world. They are cornering it, so to speak, from different sides. Since they all seem to be about equally adequate we cannot dispense with any of them until a definitely superior hypothesis should appear. A combination of them into a single eclectic hypothesis, which arbitrarily selects what somebody believes to be "the best" out of each, distorts and mangles the structure of the evidence, and the total result is weaker than if we make a frank acceptance of the four alternative theories. The evidence is clear only when one type of structural corroboration is adhered to at a time. We found, therefore, that we obtained our clearest evidence of the nature of our world by holding these four as alternative hypotheses each with its own consistent method of structural corroboration. Each could be carried so far that there was a high probability of its revealing some pretty important side of any subject in which we might be interested.

As a practical procedure for finding out all that structural corroboration could give us at present on any subject, I suggested that each of these world hypotheses should be approached separately for its judgment on the subject. We thus get the evidence clearly in the light of each of these hypotheses for the subject in hand. These four judgments may be quite different, or some or all of them may come out about the same. If the subject is a complicated one such as ours on aesthetic criticism, the judgments are likely to be quite different. The array of these separate judgments then constitutes the best clear summary of our knowledge on the subject. But for practical purposes we wish to make use of all of these judgments at once, for example, in determining whether an object has aesthetic significance or not, and, if so, how much. For practical purposes, then, I recommended what might be called a reasonable and postrational eclecticism, a synthesis of these four rational judgments in whatever way our practical good sense indicates will make the most of all of them. It amounts to a recommendation to use our common sense on our refined rational findings *after* we have clearly got these findings.

Why not use our common sense to begin with? We do. And that is explained in *World Hypotheses,* also. All of our knowledge comes out of common sense. But common sense previous to cognitive self-criticism is blind, full of unacknowledged and uncontrolled contradictions, variable, freakish, and cognitively unreliable. Cognitive refinement in the analysis of evidence by means of the multiplicative and structural modes of corroboration which we have been examining comes about just to resolve the difficulties in which irrational common sense always eventually finds itself, comes to open our eyes to the errors of common sense, to make us rational and reliable in our judgments. Prerational common sense is always with us, and is itself through its unsatisfactory irrationality the source of our rationality. It is no substitute for rationality. On the other hand, rationality unfertilized by common sense becomes sterile and dry and ultimately dogmatic. Uncompromising rationality is a serious criticism of any practical doctrine. If it is uncompromisingly rational, it is almost surely one-sided in the present stage of our knowledge—and, in the long run, almost surely impractical because unbalanced. So, that is why I recommended a postrational reasonable common sense adjustment of the pronouncements of our rational world hypotheses.

In *World Hypotheses* the movement is up from the ambiguities and contradictions of common sense towards more and more highly refined, mutually corroborative and systematized evidence. The method is a consistent following out of the one surest thing we have learned from long human experience, which is that the only way to improve our knowledge and our evidence is to get more evidence.

It is surprising how persistent is the idea that there is some short cut to this thoroughgoing empiricism. Nearly everybody wants to think that he has insight into some ultimate truth or fact which is in no need of improvement, and that the progress of knowledge builds up from this favored incorrigible foundation. The thesis of *World Hypotheses* is that though there is plenty of good empirical knowledge, none of it can be offered with certainty as ultimate or incorrigible, and that to assume that any can, is dogmatic. The thesis of *World Hypotheses* is that better knowledge develops by the accretion of evidence out of knowledge that was not so good, and that better evidence develops by cumulative corroboration out of evidence that was less adequate. The four alternative relatively adequate world hypotheses represent simply the best organizations of evidence achieved up to the present time, and consequently the best knowledge at our disposal.

The following lectures are, in a sense, prolongations of these organizations of evidence into the field of aesthetic values and aesthetic criticism. The best evidenced criteria of criticism are obviously those with the most evidence behind them. Hence, on our analysis the strongest criteria are those supported by the relatively adequate world hypotheses. These criteria we are about to describe in detail. A critic aware of the source of these criteria may thus come to see the degree of empirical justification for the tools he uses; he will be in a position to distinguish the strong and trustworthy ones from the weak ones, those not to be trusted.

In the lectures, the weak criteria are not mentioned. By specific enumeration they would be too many to mention, but their types are not numerous. The analysis in *World Hypotheses* shows clearly by implication what they would be. Since the list might be useful, I will go over them now.

First, there are a vast number of common sense criteria that have no adequate factual justification, but still persist in belief. Among these are a quantity of superstitions, criteria that unquestionably have their roots in magic, such as notions of the perfect beauty of the circle, of the straight line, of a spiral line, of proportions reducible to simple numbers, of numerical formulas for beauty. These are not entirely unfounded. Superstitions rarely are. But there is an exaggerated belief in their aesthetic potency. The aesthetic doctrine of imitation is probably, in its origin, one of these which, however, with proper qualifications has attained a central place in one of the relatively adequate theories of criticism, namely, formism. But whenever an aesthetic criterion is urged for acceptance because of its symmetry, its neatness, its simplicity, its intrinsic appeal, it is probably specious. These appeals are not evidences of cognitive reliability. They are particularly insidious appeals to a feeling of certainty, which, as shown in *World Hypotheses*, is always cognitively suspect.

From common sense also, we are offered a great many criteria which may be justifiable in their applications to other fields, but not essentially to the aesthetic. Such are cost, size, utility, and especially many moral standards. As it turns out, all of these do acquire some aesthetic justification; not, however, because they are intrinsically aesthetic criteria, but because, according to empirically justifiable aesthetic criteria, these alien standards are in some degree correlated with the aesthetic.

Secondly, there are all those criteria which owe their justification to authority. Since authority is never an empirical justification in itself, any appeal to authority as such is cognitively unsound. Consequently, criteria which owe their support to religious dogma, or supernatural revelation, are empirically dubious. There was a time when the authority of Aristotle was thought sufficient.

From this rejection of authority in itself as a ground of justification for aesthetic criteria, it does not, of course, follow that the judgments of an expert are not to be respected. The point is that an expert such as an art critic or literary critic derives his authority not from himself but from his experience, from his long observation and analysis of the evidence. His authority is based on this evidence, which it is believed he knows better than those of less experience.

Thirdly, aesthetic criteria derived from animistic sources,

as, for instance, from fundamentalist beliefs, are empirically unjustified. Animism is one of the inadequate world hypotheses, and consequently criteria dependent upon it are themselves inadequate. There is one whole side of Ruskin that has to be rejected for this reason. Also, Tolstoy's criticism is vitiated by its dependence on a washed out animism. His *What Is Art?* boils down to an appeal to judge art by certain religious criteria which he enunciates in *What Is Religion?* These latter turn out to be thin conceptualizations of animism. We can respect him for the tone of sincerity and seriousness that runs through his book, and for his contempt of those who find in art only frivolity and luxury values, and for his insistence on criteria of value that run deeper than pleasure. But he had no empirically adequate conceptions of these criteria.

Fourthly, aesthetic criteria derived from mystical sources are empirically unjustifiable. For mysticism is also one of the inadequate world hypotheses. Many artists have a strong penchant for mysticism, and the literature of criticism is full of more or less veiled appeals to the mystic intuition. Plotinus is, of course, the outstanding occidental exponent of mysticism in philosophy and aesthetics. But to see it at close hand and in contemporary garb, one may go to Yeats' critical writings. Mysticism in criticism is an appeal to depth of emotion as a value criterion in art, and it has served a useful purpose in balancing off rationalistic tendencies, and also hedonism which, for all its stress on feeling, often has a shallow way with it. But since the development of contextualistic aesthetics in recent years, there is no longer even any practical justification for mysticism in criticism. Its theoretical justification has always been meager in comparison with other available world hypotheses.

If then, to summarize, we are on our guard against types of criteria that rest their claims on common sense and the closely allied appeals to certainty and self-evidence and tradition and other ways of taking things for granted, and against those that rest their claims on authority not backed by evidence, and those that rest on animism and mysticism, which are very inadequate world hypotheses, we may be reasonably confident that our critical criteria have a large amount of evidence behind them. And, in fact, the remaining, highly corroborated criteria will turn out to be the very ones we are about to examine, those which have the support of the most adequate world hypotheses developed up to the present time.

It follows that good criticism is, as stated at the outset, criticism based on a good philosophy. For a good philosophy is simply the best disposition of all evidence available.

There is just one more preliminary point to make, which does not seem to have come out prominently enough in the lectures. That is that there is no substitute for an intimate knowledge of whatever the field of art under criticism. Though a critic can give reliable criticism only with reliable criteria of judgment, a knowledge of reliable aesthetic criteria does not guarantee good criticism. A màn must also be well acquainted with the field criticized. He must first perceive what he is judging before he can judge responsibly.

A thoroughly competent critic is one who has both intimate experience with the art he is judging and possession of reliable criteria of criticism. He may or may not be conscious of the grounds on which his criteria are supported, just as a man who uses a tool may or may not know how it is manufactured. With the tools of criticism, it seems best for the men who use them to know how they are made and to be able to judge if they are well made. There are too many fake instruments of criticism on the market. Yet many good critics do not seem ever to have examined the tools they use. By the chance of a good tradition or a good teacher they picked up a good instrument and got good results. But the greatest critics, I think, have made an effort to examine their tools and have done something that amounted to showing their source of justification in one of the relatively adequate world hypotheses. This is notably true of Coleridge and Pater.

Much creditable criticism is of a sort that might be called technical, pointing out means of attaining certain artistic aims which an artist may or may not have employed to best advantage, assuming that he had those aims. Intimate experience with a technique is sufficient for this type of criticism, and it is sound if the technique happens to be aesthetically justified, and if the work of art under consideration happens to come under the aim for which the technique is a means. But such criticism is at the mercy of a tradition, and the narrowness of such criticism is likely to show up even where it actually applies. Really sound and understanding criticism has to go beyond this. It actually has to have its sources in the best and in the most that we know, and this is what I try to explain in the beginning lecture.

If a critic has plenty of intimate experience with his art and is conscious of the nature and action of those aesthetic criteria which are empirically most adequately supported, his judgments cannot go far wrong and his influence on the public and also eventually on artists is bound to be beneficial. This is scarcely to be disputed. The only element of novelty in the standpoint of these lectures is the thesis that there are at present a number of equally adequate criteria, which need to be kept in mind and adjusted to one another for a full understanding of the aesthetic value either of a single work, or of an artist's total achievement. There are a number—for these criteria are empirical and have the status of hypotheses, and the evidence is not yet decisive as to what, beyond all likelihood of subsequent revision, are the ultimate criteria of aesthetic value.

1

A Theory of Empirical Criticism

THE PURPOSE of these lectures is to seek out the factual grounds of criticism in the arts. I shall pass over the skeptical idea that there are no grounds of criticism. It appears pretty obvious that there are, in view of the gathering literature on the subject. Where there is much intellectual turmoil there is almost sure to be something to stir up the commotion. But beyond that, whenever the skeptical point of view is probed to its roots, we unearth some idea to the effect that judgments of art are entirely matters of personal preference, to which is added the *non sequitur* that therefore there is no factual basis for the judgments.

This last is an astonishing addition when we think about it. As if human preferences were not facts, and as if they did not have a firm basis in the structures of human behavior and the human mind. It is this very view, as it happens, with which I plan in the next lecture to begin: the view that the worth of a work of art or of an experience of beauty consists in its being an object of men's preferences, likings, satisfactions, pleasures. I shall call it the naturalistic, or, more unambiguously, the mechanistic theory of criticism.

But first I want to tell something about the method of approach to this subject which I propose to use in these lectures. It is an empirical method. Anything that rests on an *a priori*, or upon claims of self-evidence, or upon uncorroborated authority; anything offered without evidence or with claims be-

yond a reasonable probability on the basis of the evidence, in
short, anything dogmatic is rejected. One wonders what else
would be done with such claims. But they creep into critical
inquiries in the strangest guises. In any guise or disguise they
are rejected. The judgments of criticism I shall be seeking
will be based on facts. They will be factual judgments of a
certain kind purporting to be true. Being empirical judgments,
however, they will not claim to be certain, but only probable
to a degree justified by the evidence.

If the idea that sound criticism is a question of fact appears
strange to anyone, I recommend that he ask himself why. He
may find that he is harboring one of those dogmas in disguise
about which I was just speaking, that he is assuming criticism
needs no empirical proof or is not susceptible to proof. There
are so many ways in which men have made such assumptions
plausible to themselves that it is useless to try to list them. The
way that applies to the next man will be another way not
thought of before. I merely want here to indicate a symptom
of dogmatism in the sphere of aesthetic criticism. If anyone
finds it queer that evaluations of the beauty of things should
be judgments of fact, subject to error, he is probably nourish-
ing some dogmatic presuppositions. He may be just confused.
But probably he is protecting some assumptions which he has
never exposed to the light of full evidence.

Our method is a way of seeking out the full evidence. What,
then, is the evidence on which aesthetic criticism rests? Here
is some of it: There is first the evidence of history as this is
summarized in histories of art, histories of criticism, histories
of aesthetics. There is second the evidence of the nature of
cultural objects, of which works of art are examples, as these
are described in anthropology and studies of civilization. There
is third need of some reference to the evidence of the nature
of physical objects, since works of art are physical objects
and chiefly as physical objects acquire that permanency for

perception so often stressed in aesthetic theory. Lastly there is emphatic need for the evidence of the nature of mind, since the aesthetic experience draws heavily on emotion, memory, perception, imagination, and, in fact, on every major topic of psychological investigation.

History, anthropology, social theory, physics, psychology, and really also biology are all involved. We might as well include the rest of our knowledge, and say that sound judgment in art is such a judgment as is compatible with all the knowledge we have; or that it is the application of all the knowledge we have to objects in the aesthetic field.

You might think that it would require a superman to bring the results of all our knowledge to bear on the objects of a special field. But actually we have ways within the capacity of ordinary human minds for doing this. The structure of knowledge as a whole has been a human interest for many centuries; and, what are often called philosophies but might better be called world hypotheses have been worked up by men who have made comprehensive understanding a major pursuit. These philosophies are hypotheses about how all available evidence shapes up. Though the world hypotheses of individual philosophers differ in detail, these individual hypotheses divide into rather clearly defined groups often called schools of philosophy. Each school amounts to a single world hypothesis within which goes on much discussion of detail. Such discussions of detail are minor issues. The big issues over the nature of knowledge and the organization of evidence go on between the schools, between the integral world hypotheses. If, then, anyone wants to apply the whole weight of our knowledge to any specific field, the way he can do this is to direct these world hypotheses upon the subject matter of his field and see what the results are.

The results are not likely to be entirely harmonious. There are at present probably four such world hypotheses worthy

of consideration. I am going to call them mechanism, contextualism, organicism, and formism. They are (when all
dogmatic elements are removed) four ways of putting together the mass of empirical evidence that man has gathered
up from all sources. It is as if we had a heap of jigsaw shapes
which look as if they should go together to form a consistent
picture. We found them scattered about the attic. We are
pretty sure that a good many of the shapes are missing, and
that some of them have been split and broken, and that probably all of them are nicked and worn. Now, a cynical person
can very well say that these cannot be put together at all, and
that the pieces that do fit perfectly together do so only by a
kind of chance from which nothing can be inferred about
the pieces belonging together, and that as for order there is
just as much order in the pieces jumbled up in a heap on the
floor as fitted together with all their boundaries matching,
since an order is just an arrangement, and there is no basis of
choice among arrangements except convenience or an aesthetic
whim on the part of the player manipulating the pieces. Such
a person today goes by the name of a logical positivist. I do
not mean that all logical positivists take this attitude, but that
many do, and that today this attitude is closely associated with
the men of this school.

This is not a place to examine the dogmas implied in such an
attitude. But even superficially it is apparent that a man who
refuses to accept the evidence of any connectivity among data
is just as dogmatic as one who refuses to accept evidence
against some pet view of connectivity. Actual positivists, to be
sure, rarely make such a denial and are shocked at the accusa-
tion. They talk about correlations. They insist that they accept
correlations as these are established and confirmed by observation and experiment. But "correlation" is an ambiguous word
and may conveniently now refer only to conjunctions in human experience and now to inferences from constant conjunctions in perception to connections in nature. The positivist's

favorite way of denying the inferences is to ask a rhetorical question: "What does it add to an observed constant conjunction of sensory observations to say that these are evidences of connections of fact in nature?" The answer is supposed to be, obviously, "Nothing." But the answer would appear to me to be: "The difference between being legitimately able to make predictions and other inferences on the basis of the observations and not being able to." If one arrangement of the jigsaw shapes is as good as any other and it is only a matter of a player's interest whether he piles them up in a tower or fits them together on a table, then no inferences can be made from shape to shape. But if the pieces do belong together and a gap appears among a group of pieces that fit edge to edge together on a table, then an inference can be made that a piece the shape of the gap is missing.

Now, I hold that it is not empirical to neglect the evidence for the connectivity of facts in nature. Admittedly there is some risk in making an hypothesis as to the manner of this connectivity. For any hypothesis is an inference and inferences are fallible. My position is that there is a preponderance of evidence for connections of fact in nature but that the precise manner of the connections is open to hypothesis. Hypotheses particularly concerned with these connections I call world hypotheses. The positivists' attempt to ignore these hypotheses amounts to a denial of this preponderance of evidence for connections of fact in nature. This attempt of theirs, moreover, boomerangs upon these positivists themselves, since in fact whenever they commit themselves to constructive writing sustained enough to exhibit their preconceptions, it is generally not hard to show that they presuppose the categories of one or another of the very world hypotheses which they sought to ignore. A frank acceptance of the presuppositions of world hypotheses in extended empirical thought is more empirical than a neglect of them. Nothing less is fully empirical.

So this is why in seeking out the empirical basis of art

criticism I ask you to follow through with me the bearing of
the four world hypotheses which have been most successful up
to the present time in organizing the materials of human knowledge and thereby giving grounds for inferring the connections
of fact that exist in nature. A study of the way these four
world hypotheses handle aesthetic materials will give us as
broad and balanced an aesthetic judgment as our knowledge
to date makes possible.

The first step in our method, then, is an acknowledgment of
the empirical bearing of world hypotheses in the determination of empirically justifiable aesthetic judgments.

Then what we next want to do is to find the aesthetic field
to which we wish to apply these several world hypotheses.
A momentarily disconcerting problem arises here because
these world hypotheses connect up the facts of nature in
somewhat different ways. Being hypotheses about the manner
of connections of fact in nature, they would not be different
hypotheses unless they did discriminate many of these connections in different ways. It is not surprising, then, to discover that the boundaries of the aesthetic field, as these are
traced out in accord with the categories of the four hypotheses, do not exactly coincide. How, then, can we determine
that we are dealing with essentially the same factual material
as we pass from the aesthetic descriptions of one of these
hypotheses to those of another?

This problem has been solved in the practice of philosophers
over many generations, though the significance of the practice
has not till recently been noticed. The test of congruence in
this situation is an appeal to common sense. In the aesthetic
field, for instance, it is generally acknowledged that the poems,
pictures, statues, musical compositions of the great artists are
aesthetic materials, and also many buildings such as the
medieval cathedrals, and fondly made tools like the paddles
and baskets and pottery of primitive peoples, and dance and

ritual, and also certain perceptions of nature like the sea and starry nights and sunsets and pleasant pastures and groves and sometimes fear-inspiring scenes like storms and mountains and waterfalls. This is the sort of material from which writers of aesthetics, whatever their school, have drawn their illustrations and to which they have made their appeal for the acceptance of their views. To deny that these are works of art or objects of beauty would be regarded by most men as contrary to common sense. As objects and experiences commonly denoted as beautiful or aesthetic these may be taken as the common ostensive reference of these terms. Hereby we have a common sense ostensive definition of the aesthetic field. It is by reference to this ostensive definition of the field that the various refined analyses of the field in the perspectives of the various world hypotheses are known to be congruent. If two different descriptions purporting to be descriptions of the aesthetic field do in fact refer to the field denoted above, then we take them to be alternative descriptions of the same field.

Such a definition, it must be stressed, is only a *test definition* of the field. Occasionally men have sought to set such a definition in a normative rôle, to make it the criterion of aesthetic values in reference to which other judgments of aesthetic value should be corrected. But this cannot be justified. For one of the main problems of aesthetic judgment is the justification of the definition of the field. The common sense field is not as such justified at all. It is simply taken for granted. To employ it as a norm is consequently to use it as a basis of aesthetic judgment without empirical justification; in other words, dogmatically. It is, in fact, a very vaguely defined field, and as soon as a precise description is given of it, the original common sense denotations are superseded. This result is one that is simply noted. A common sense definition is invaluable as a test definition of the congruence of competing more refined definitions of the field. It is totally unsuited to be a criterion of judgment over the field.

The recognition of this test definition of the aesthetic field is, then, our second step. Our third step in this procedure towards getting empirical criteria of aesthetic judgment would now be to develop as precise descriptions as possible of the denoted field in accordance with the categories of each of the four relatively adequate world hypotheses. This step will occupy us in the four succeeding lectures. I will try in each instance to show just how the particular description of the field develops out of the categories of the relevant world hypothesis. In doing this, I shall naturally have to ask you to assume the empirical justification of the world hypotheses themselves. And yet the descriptions of the field are not really deductions from the world hypotheses. Our procedure is not the objectionable "aesthetics from above" decried by Fechner. The descriptions are made directly from the materials of the aesthetic field. What is determined by the world hypotheses which guide the descriptions is the proper limits of the field in terms of the attitude taken towards the facts. The facts are described as nearly as possible as they are found. But it cannot be denied that perceptions of fact are affected by the attitude taken toward them, and the empirical problem is to have this attitude controlled by confirmatory facts and not by arbitrary bias. This is the control, and the only control, that a world hypothesis can legitimately have over factual materials. Being different hypotheses of the way the facts of the world fit together, they will inevitably arrange these facts somewhat differently one from another, and may even disagree as to the interpretation of some of the facts themselves. But nothing is done to aesthetic materials by a world hypothesis except to fit them in with other empirical materials, and, in doing so, to determine the feasible or the natural boundaries of the aesthetic field. This determination is the basis of all aesthetic judgment.

If, then, the third step is a description of the materials of the aesthetic field in terms of each world hypothesis, the fourth is to define this field in accordance with the descriptions. The definition so obtained is the fundamental criterion of aesthetic judgment, fundamental because it determines what is or what is not an aesthetic fact. For the most damning judgment that can be made of any object which purports to be an aesthetic fact is the privative judgment that this object is not an aesthetic fact, that it falls outside the field altogether, that, for instance, a Brancusi is not sculpture, a Picasso not painting, an Amy Lowell or an Alexander Pope not poetry, a Corbusier not architecture, and so on. Such judgments are applications of one or another definition of the aesthetic field held by the critic, and the empirical legitimacy of these judgments depends on the empirical justification of the definition. (Needless to say, I regard all the judgments above as empirically unjustified.)

It has rather recently been discovered that definitions are the ultimate basis of judgments of value. Men used to think of norms as the basis, which was right enough except that norms have to be defined; or they would think of authority as the basis, such as the fiat of an expert, or a deity, or a man's inner aesthetic taste, which again, however, required a definition to indicate the expert, the deity, or the bounds of aesthetic taste. We now clearly see that the basis of the whole matter is a definition.

But at just the same time that we have discovered that definitions are the ultimate basis of judgments of value, we have also become conscious of the fact that definitions regularly involve an arbitrary factor. Many recent writers have become so excessively conscious of this fact that they have excluded every empirical reference from a definition. They distinguish a definition from a proposition by a flat dichotomy. A definition, they say, is a rule establishing the meaning of a symbol and is neither true nor false; a proposition is a statement that is true or false. The implication is that a definition is never controlled by the truth or falsity of its symbolic references and presumably never has empirical references. If any such references can be found among the symbols of a definition, they are entirely accidental, and not essential to the function of a definition.

Now let me say emphatically that this narrow, rigid, and arbitrary definition of definition will not do at all for a basis of evaluation in value theory. It is essential that a definition which is to be used as the ultimate basis of judgments of value, should be responsible to the relevant facts. When a definition of the aesthetic field is being constructed, this is done with the intent that it shall yield true judgments of what are or are not aesthetic materials and of the degrees of aesthetic value these materials contain. Such a criterion cannot have any significance unless it is in close contact with the empirical materials out of which it originates and unless it is continuously controlled by those materials. In short, it is an intrinsic function of a definition employed as a criterion of value that it should contain a truth reference to the materials over which it is to legislate.

This is not to deny that there is an arbitrary element in such a definition containing a truth reference, and that this arbitrary element is what differentiates the expression from a proposition. But the arbitrariness is reduced to the very minimum of declaring that, for instance, the term "aesthetic" (or whatever synonym one wishes) shall signify such and such a combination of characters, in so far as they truly describe the facts of a specified field. It is, in other words, a part of the contract in framing the definition, that if the references to the empirical field on the basis of which the definition was constructed prove false, the definition will be modified or abandoned. In this way the definition is rendered responsible to the facts and is empirically secure. Otherwise, the definition would be completely arbitrary and irresponsible and totally unfit for its function as a basic criterion of value.

In order to show explicitly what I mean, let me contrast three types of definition, all of which we shall make use of in the course of these lectures—the ostensive definition, and what I shall call the equational definition, and what I shall call the descriptive. The first two are dyadic—that is, involve only two terms—the third is triadic and involves three.

An ostensive definition may be symbolized this way:

$$S \quad \frac{\text{indicates}}{\text{is ostensively defined by}} \quad O$$

The symbol to be defined, S, indicates by some agency such as pointing, an object, or group of objects, or type of object. The symbol is thereby said to be defined by that object. Thus the meaning of a proper name is ordinarily defined by introducing (a polite way of pointing at) the person who has it. We have just now ostensively defined the field of aesthetic value for common sense by naming sample objects in the field. Also a description of an operation may indicate a type of object. For instance, I can define the word "pain" by telling you to take a pin and stick it into your skin quite hard, and what you will feel will be pain. We shall employ this kind of ostensive definition quite often in these lectures for we are all the time having to name facts of immediacy in aesthetic discussion and this can only be done ostensively.

An equational definition can be symbolized this way:

$$S \quad \frac{\text{is equated with}}{\text{is equationally defined by}} \quad UV$$

The symbol to be defined, S, is equated with a group of other symbols, UV, which define it, so that it can stand for the group. Its purpose is solely one of convenience and of assistance to clarity of thought. The symbol defined can then be substituted for the symbol group that defines it wherever the latter appears. Neither the page nor the mind is then cluttered up with a lot of unnecessary symbols during an operation of thought.

We shall constantly have use for the equational definition. For instance, presently I shall define a standard as a quantitative criterion. This is a purely equational definition and has no reference to fact. It saves me the necessity of using two long words where one will do.

The equational definition is the typical definition of mathematics, and, since mathematical thought is a model of clear thinking, the transition is easy to the idea that the method of constructing definitions in mathematics should be accepted as the model for all definitions. This, however, does not follow for the reason that mathematics and likewise logic, so far as the latter relates to analytical and deductive processes only, are not concerned with references to fact. In other words, the equational definition is a model only for thought that has no explicit reference to fact. It is liable to misuse, that is, to fallacious consequences, if it is taken as a model for definition in empirical thought.

Here, for instance, is the sort of thing that can be done—is frequently done—with the equational definition. A writer takes a quick survey of an empirical field and notes a rough correlation between the common sense use of, let us say, "value" and feelings of satisfaction. He then constructs an equational definition and equates the symbol "value" with symbols referring to what he has observed. He makes the equation:

$$\text{Value} = \text{satisfaction of impulse}$$

He maintains that he has asserted nothing. He has simply given precision to his thought. But then he proceeds to accumulate observations and develop a theory of value on the basis of his definition. Presently you will find him asserting that what men really mean by value is satisfaction of impulse. Since several thousand words have intervened between the statement of his definition as a mere analytical convenience and his assertion of it as a true hypothesis, the reader is likely to overlook the transition. The writer will appear to have proved his theory.

Now if another writer, B, comes along and after his survey of the empirical field says that he thinks that value is not primarily a matter of satisfaction but is a relation of interest taken in objects, or is the capacity of a situation to satisfy interest, or is integration of interests, or is a condition of adjustment to one's environment, then writer A suavely says, "But I have already defined value as satisfaction of impulse, and it is logically confusing for other men to employ the term with other meanings. I am not sure that I know what they are talking about, nor am I sure that they do. But if there are facts corresponding to their ideas, they are not facts of value as I have defined it." In other words, he sticks to his definition in spite of the facts, and wants you to accept his theory because he can define it clearly and has found a few facts that apply to it. This is the modern way of the *a priori*. It is the new sort of ontological argument.

If at last writer B does corner A and seems to have shown him the fallacy of his ways, and that he has been trying to put over an empirical theory by definition, A's rejoinder is very likely to be, "Why, I never ascribed truth to my definition. I have always insisted on the distinction between definitions and propositions. I was simply making clear my use of the term and exhibiting its application." The fault is all B's. A is as innocent as his equational definition. But now, you notice, A disclaims responsibility for his treatment of the facts.

Do you now see why I advocate a kind of definition which is expressly responsible to the facts, whenever a definition is to be employed for factual purposes? This sort of responsibility is guaranteed by the form of definition which I am calling descriptive. It has a triadic structure, as follows:

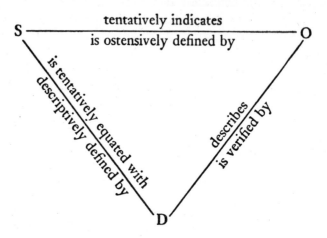

Here S is the symbol to be defined, O the object or field of objects empirically to be defined, and D the description of the objects which constitutes the definition of S. The descriptive definition is a sort of combination of the ostensive and equational but is not reducible to them. They neither of them contain the descriptive reference of D to O which is essential to the descriptive definition. Moreover, the equational definition equates the symbol S with finality to a symbol group such as the words of the description D, whereas in the descriptive definition the equating is tentative and subject to the verification of the description. It follows that the description, D, may be changed through a succession of approximations, without changing S which refers steadily to O. Moreover, the indicative reference of S to O may also be adjusted in the light of the description, D. This process is known as redefining a term to make the definition of it more precise and closer to the facts. It is the familiar process of fitting an hypothesis to the facts. Strictly speaking, an equational definition is incapable of redefinition since the symbol to be defined is flatly equated with the defining symbol group. The descriptive definition is not rigid but adaptable to the facts, and by the constant reference of the symbol S to the facts O, the descriptive definition is held steadily responsible to the facts.

This is certainly what we want when a definition is to be employed as a criterion of judgment in human values.

Technically speaking, a descriptive definition is not a proposition and is not true or false. This trait is what makes it properly a definition. For the relating of S to D and to O is arbitrary. But as a triadic structure, it contains a truth reference, since it contains the relation of D to O which is a verificatory reference. Elliptically we may speak of a descriptive definition as true (or false). But strictly speaking it is an arbitrary determination of the meaning of a symbol in terms of a symbol group, subject, however, to the verifiability of the symbol group in terms of certain indicated facts. The proviso in this case that the defining symbol groups be verifiable is contained within the definitional rule.

I am sure you will understand why I have taken all this time on the subject of definition. When one first discovers that the primary criterion of judgments of aesthetic, and also moral, value is a definition, it appears as if we had turned the whole matter over to the arbitration of words. Then it looks as if it were all a question of *mere* definition and of mere preference on the part of the definer as to how he likes to use words. To make things worse, many logicians and philosophers have lent their authority and given aid and succor to this way of looking at the matter by defining definition as the equational definition. They have used their new way of the *a priori* on definition. I trust I have made the fallacy of their new way of the *a priori* sufficiently clear to you, and have been able to regain for you a justifiable confidence in the empirical use of definition. I wanted you to see that the descriptive definition is not arbitrary in any sense but the selection of the symbol to be defined. The definition itself is held responsible to the facts indicated throughout, and is empirically as reliable as our knowledge of the facts can make it.

There is, of course, a long tradition in logic of a distinction between real and verbal definitions. Those who wish to give up the distinction are, I believe, acting precipitately and without a sufficiently wide view of the function of definitions in the full range of human activity. It is essential for some definitions, in order that they may fulfill the functions for which they are formed, to contain a truth reference. These are what the traditional logicians had in mind when they wrote of real definitions. A better term, so as not to bring up some ancient Aristotelian issues, is, as I have suggested, the descriptive definition.

Our fourth step, then, is to frame a descriptive definition of the aesthetic field for each world hypothesis. This is the fundamental criterion of aesthetic judgment for the view concerned. This gives us the qualitative judgment of what is or is not aesthetic. Quantitative standards are directly developed out of this definitional criterion by noting what quantitative factors there are among the characters of the definition which describe the aesthetic field. Since these standards are derived immediately from the definition which is derived from a description of the relevant facts, these standards are as firmly based empirically as the definition itself.

The four steps of our method, then, are these:

1. The acknowledgment of world hypotheses as tentative organizations of the totality of evidence, the most adequate of these affording the most probable conceptions available of the interconnections of the facts of the world.

2. The acceptance of a common sense ostensive definition of the field of aesthetic facts as a *test definition* for determining

the congruence of the more highly refined definitions developed through the application of the categories of world hypotheses to the analysis of the field.

3. Descriptions of the foregoing field as this field appears in the perspective of the relatively adequate world hypotheses. In principle, this means that these descriptions receive the benefit of corroboration with other descriptions of fact developed by these same hypotheses in other fields.

4. The setting up of definitions of the aesthetic field in accordance with the foregoing descriptions. These definitions constitute the basic criteria of aesthetic judgment, determining what is or is not an aesthetic object or experience. Quantitative standards are derived by noting the quantitative characters contained in the terms of the definitions.[1]

The types of criteria of judgment that come to light by this method and their relation to each other are then the following:

A. Definition—as the *qualitative* criterion of aesthetic judgment determining what is or is not an aesthetic value and whether its value is positive or negative.

B. Intrinsic Standards—as *quantitative* criteria determining the amount of aesthetic value. There are as many standards as there are characters with quantitative dimensions contained in the complete descriptive definition of the field. These standards are guaranteed as relevant to the field in that they are simply quantifications of the characters of the description. Standards are therefore derived from definitions: the quantitative criteria come from the qualitative. (If a definition gen-

---

[1] Steps two, three, and four, it may be noticed, correspond to the three references contained in the descriptive definition. For, in step two, the ostensive test definition of common sense gives us the indicative reference for the term "aesthetic value" to the field of facts. In step three, the descriptions of this field give us the descriptive reference. There are to be several alternative descriptions of the field in the present study, but we have seen how the descriptive definition provides for this as part of its tentative and empirical character. In step four, aesthetic values are tentatively equated with these definitions.

erates several standards, these are likely to be gathered together into a group and called "the standard" for that definition. So people speak of "the hedonistic standard" though
pleasure has several dimensions of quantity.)

C. Extrinsic Criteria—in addition to a descriptive definition and
its intrinsic standards there are always a lot of properties
roughly correlated with the definitional properties and so
roughly indicative of the aesthetic value of an object. These
may suitably be called extrinsic criteria. They are for the
most part the various techniques and forms of composition
conducive to the production of aesthetic value. There is, as
might be expected, more general agreement about the extrinsic criteria than the intrinsic. Moreover, criteria that are
intrinsic for one descriptive definition of the field are very
likely to be accepted as extrinsic for another. But the extrinsic criteria nevertheless depend upon the intrinsic for
their justification.

With these considerations of method behind us, we shall
now proceed to apply this method through the four relatively
adequate world hypotheses already mentioned. I shall devote
a lecture to each one of the four views, and shall emphasize
and perhaps overemphasize the particular bent of each view
in its way of dealing with aesthetic materials. This will have
the effect of making the views more divergent than they
might appear to be in the practice of some of their exponents.
But since we are more interested here in becoming aware of
the particular flavor and contribution of these different points
of view than in trying to make any one of them do for all
(which actually is impossible), we shall not go amiss to emphasize the contrasts rather than the similarities.

When all is done, and we have seen the aesthetic judgment
in the light of these four views separately, I shall show how
they can all work together in practice and then briefly
construct a synthetic definition which will bring together the
contributions of all four. It will be workable in the light of
them all severally, and will be understandable in the recollec-

tion of their distinct perspectives, but like some of Cezanne's pictures which combine several eye-levels in a single composition, it will sacrifice consistency for richness. Yet, if we accept this synthetic definition not superficially as a final epitome of the truth about aesthetic judgment, but rather as a complex symbol of the bearing of four relevant perspectives on the field, each of which needs to be taken into account in the present stage of our knowledge in order to obtain a balanced judgment of any aesthetic object, we shall not go far astray.

2

Mechanistic Criticism

THAT PLEASURE is good and pain is bad is generally taken as fact not to be doubted without ridicule, so evident as to need no further evidence. On this datum the mechanistic theory of criticism is based. The only question that ordinarily occurs to a mechanist in aesthetics is how most feasibly to distinguish aesthetic pleasure from other kinds.

Nevertheless, granting that the mechanistic theory of value acquires a particular force through the immediacy of this datum such as no other theory can boast, we have only to remember Calvinistic and Kantian ideas of the wickedness or the lowliness of lives of pleasure to realize that a theory which finds the ultimate basis of value in pleasure and pain does require corroboration and defense.

The line of the defense consists in demonstrating that value cannot plausibly be located outside of individuals within whom pleasures and pains generate. Show that these feelings occur inside human organisms, and that these organisms are bounded so that the feelings cannot get out, and the proof is complete. Now the mechanistic world hypothesis organizes its evidence in a manner that produces precisely this result. It is the only relatively adequate hypothesis that does so.

Though the structure of this theory is familiar, it will pay us swiftly to follow it through in its present bearing. Its basic category is the space-time field, in which the locational or geometrical character is highly emphasized. The structure of the space-time field is the ground plan of the universe, and nothing is real that has not a location in physical space-time. "Only particulars exist" is a basic mechanistic idea, together with the corollary that what makes anything particular is having a local habitation, a place and a time or a place-time.

Mass, charge, and other properties are located relatively to one another in this field, forming clusters of properties which constitute elementary substances. Some form of physical atomism is thus characteristic of mechanism, and the form of this atomism described for our times is the familiar hierarchy of subatomic elements, chemical atoms, molecules, cells, and organisms. The higher level entities are described as combinations of lower level entities, but the entities on any one level are separate entities with their own locations in the space-time field and their own autonomy. That is, any chemical atom always has its spatio-temporal location distinct from any other chemical atom and has its own specific ways of acting upon and responding to other chemical atoms. So on up and down the line. The universe is thus conceived as a huge aggregation or system of essentially separate individuals. These individuals have specific potentialities of association. But the form of an association of individuals never actually takes over the autonomy of the individuals that make it up. Each chemical atom has its own valency and affinities, whether or not it combines with other atoms.

Now, the bearing of the foregoing on our problem is that this conception of the way in which the evidence shapes up in the fields of physics, chemistry, and biology firmly supports the view of a man as an autonomous human individual with certain capacities of association; that is, as essentially a biological organism with a place of his own in the universe and bounded pretty definitely by his skin. On this view, it would be absurd to think of human values as basically determined by anything outside a man's skin. An individualistic theory of value is indicated by every item of evidence in a mechanistic world.

It should be added that on the mechanistic view there is no clear evidence of consciousness and of the thoughts, images, conations, and feelings that go with it, outside the level of biological organisms, and there has even been a tendency to question the existence of consciousness outside the behavior of human organisms. The elements of consciousness are usually regarded as correlated with certain physiological activities of organisms, so that an identification of value with feeling inevitably places value within the bodies of biological organisms and possibly only within the bodies of human organisms. Hence, one man's feeling cannot possibly be another man's feeling. There is no literal community of feeling possible on a mechanistic view. I may feel badly about your toothache. But my sympathetic pain is my own pain in my own body spatially separated from the pain of your toothache which is your own pain in your own body. Feelings on a mechanistic view are radically individualistic. Furthermore, and this cannot be too much stressed, it is the insulation of the bodies spatially separated from each other that guarantees the individuality of the feelings—guarantees, in other words, that mechanistic descriptions of value will not slip off outside of bodies. For if a man is located in his body and his own activities are limited to the activities of his body, he will have no values unless these are to be found in the activities of his body. So, that is where values in mechanism are definitely located and held.

With this general background let us see how some outstanding mechanistic writer on aesthetics goes about locating the field of aesthetic value within the mechanistic categories. Mechanistic aesthetics and criticism—pleasure aesthetics—has had a long and vigorous history, especially in the English empirical tradition. Its main line stems from Hobbes thence to Locke and the associationists, producing a large number of influential literary critics in the last quarter of the eighteenth century and culminating in Walter Pater in the nineteenth. The maturest systematic treatments of this aesthetic approach were brought out even later, among which Santayana's *Sense of Beauty*[1] and Prall's *Aesthetic Judgment*[2] seem to me the outstanding works. Though these two books differ considerably in their handling of details and in their degree of consistency to a mechanistic background, they are noticeably similar in structure, both beginning with the sensory materials of art, that is, with the elements of beauty, the aesthetic atoms, so to speak, thence proceeding to the composition of these in orders or forms, and finally to added accretions which these attract to themselves by association in the mode of expression — and the two books are also similar in their tone, in a pervading sensuousness and fineness of sensuous discrimination. For in this is the genius of mechanistic criticism fostered by the categorial structure of the world hypothesis which supports it. Pater exhibits this same sensuous sensibility to an even higher degree.   .

I choose Santayana to follow in his derivation of the aesthetic field, since he is more explicit than Prall, and keeps, I feel, closer to the implications of the mechanistic categories. He derives the aesthetic field by a series of exclusions. After acknowledging the control of the common sense test definition by remarking that "the sphere of critical and appreciative perception is, roughly speaking, what we are dealing with, . . . the perception of values,"[3] he draws his first circle about an area that he knows is much too large but contains what he is hunting for—namely, the field of the whole

[1] George Santayana, *The Sense of Beauty* (New York: C. Scribner's Sons, 1896).
[2] David Wright Prall, *Aesthetic Judgment* (New York: Thomas Y. Crowell Company, 1929).
[3] *The Sense of Beauty*, p. 10.

mechanical world. And he points out that in so far as such a world contains no consciousness, it contains no value. As a *reductio ad absurdum* he pictures the world as if it contained no consciousness.

In such a world there might have come to be the most perfect organization. . . . But the particles of matter would have remained unconscious of their collocation, and all nature would have been insensible of their changing arrangement. We only, the possible spectators of that process, by virtue of our own interests and habits, could see any progress or culmination in it. . . . But apart from ourselves, and our human bias, we can see in such a mechanical world no element of value whatever. In removing consciousness, we have removed the possibility of worth.[4]

So only where consciousness is, will value be. But consciousness might be entirely intellectual, and still no value would appear. "Every event would then be noted, its relations would be observed, its recurrence might even be expected; but all this would happen without a shadow of desire, of pleasure, or of regret." So Santayana draws the circle still closer and excludes the rational. "Values," he says, "spring

[4] *The Sense of Beauty*, p. 17. Though I agree with Santayana's procedure in determining the locus of value for a mechanistic theory, I should not admit that this observation of his limited value for the mechanist to overt conscious manifestations of it. The evidence today for "unconscious" fears and wishes is too great to be ignored or explained away; and, if these do not actually involve "unconscious" pleasures and pains, they certainly involve "unconscious" values and would need to be provided for in any adequate mechanistic theory of value.

Few mechanistic philosophers, aside from Edwin Holt, have seriously tried to come to grips with the psychoanalytical concept of the "unconscious," though the Freudian mode of thought has a strong mechanistic trend. The very term "unconscious" is perhaps unfortunate and the material referred to should possibly have been called the "repressed" or the "unintegrated." An "unconscious" impulse is actually a repressed one, and there is no reason to think it is not qualitatively the same as an unrepressed but overtly frustrated one. Since it is repressed, the subject cannot report on it, and does not overtly know he has it. If we said he had a repressed consciousness of the impulse, would not that accurately describe the situation? If so, Santayana's position that all values involve consciousness would still hold.

from the immediate and inexplicable reaction of vital impulse, and from the irrational part of our nature." [5] Values are thus discovered in the area of life impulses and consciousness.

But not all values are aesthetic. There are also moral values. Santayana declares that these are mainly negative and always instrumental. Morality, he holds here, generally says "Don't," and if it is positive it is in "the consciousness of benefits probably involved." [6] This limited view of moral values is a hasty judgment and reflects a Puritanical influence, and is far from the spirit and tradition of hedonistic ethics as Santayana himself in his later writings abundantly confirms. Even in this book he presently says, "Evidently all values must be ultimately intrinsic," so that the ultimate aim of ethics would be to achieve a maximum of intrinsic values. Here he speaks genuinely in the spirit of hedonistic ethics. But his slip at this point in defining the moral field proves irrelevant to his derivation of the aesthetic field. For what he is actually excluding is simply instrumental and negative values, with the result that he merely demarcates for us the field of intrinsic pleasures.

But even this field Santayana regards as too large. He criticizes a couple of traditional suggestions (namely, disinterestedness and universality) for qualifying the intrinsic pleasures that are aesthetic, and finally gives as his own qualification the act of "objectification." His considered definition of the aesthetic field is then that of *objectified pleasure.* By "objectification" he means that same process applied to pleasures which we habitually apply to colors when we appear to see them as qualities on the surfaces of external objects. Colors, like all other sensations, are in Santayana's view (in strictest conformity with the evidences of mechanism) correlated with physiological activities located in the human

[5] *The Sense of Beauty,* pp. 18, 19.
[6] *Ibid.,* p. 23.

body. When, accordingly, they are perceived as if they were qualities on the surfaces of external objects, they get this apparent location by a psychological process of projection which Santayana describes in some detail following traditional descriptions of mechanistic philosophers and psychologists from Berkeley and Hume down. Colors, shapes, textures easily become objectified as a result of past experience, since they remain relatively constant in their interrelationships in perception. But pleasures and pains are variable in their association with objects, and so tend to be associated with the organism and, we might say, subjectified. When, however, a situation is such that pleasures are objectified and appear to be incorporated in an external object along with the colors and textures of the object, then this object is aesthetically perceived. What this limitation means in practice is that the spectator is so absorbed in the object that he forgets himself or loses himself in it, and all of his experience is merged into one pleasant or even ecstatic whole. There is no split then in his perception setting this much of it on one side as due to him and that much of it as due to the object. Santayana thus virtually describes the aesthetic field as that of completely absorbed pleasant experiences.

This, you see, is a description of fact. It is as fully empirical as possible with the data available. It is tied in with, and has the corroboration of a great mass of empirical description from psychology, biology, and physics. But it is also to be noted that all these descriptions are interrelated through a set of guiding concepts which have grown out of the total mass of empirical material and in some degree control the observations. In short, Santayana's description of aesthetic value is at once an empirical description and one in accordance with, and under the control of, the mechanistic world hypothesis.

This description is now implicitly set up as an aesthetic

criterion by Santayana. That is, it is converted into a definition for purposes of evaluation.

Santayana's definition has not been widely accepted by mechanistic critics and philosophers in spite of universal respect for his analysis. It will be instructive to ask why. The answer briefly is that it is too narrow, and does not coincide closely enough with the common sense test definition. It circumscribes the optimum aesthetic experience but leaves out the common acts of appreciation. Not always in reading a poem or looking at a statue or enjoying nature do we lose ourselves within the object and objectify our delight. Even in the course of appreciation of a single work like a symphony our attitude ordinarily moves in and out of the complete objectification that Santayana demands. And in all the lesser aesthetic delights of flowers in a garden, the flight of a bird, the sheen of silk, or the grace of a gesture, full objectification is rarely expected. "I like it" for these pleasures seems even to indicate a keener enjoyment than "It is delightful." Moreover, it is in these swift sensuous discriminations that the particular contribution of mechanistic criticism is made. A hedonist is particularly conscious of his body, and of all that his body receives and gives in delight. Out of an enthusiasm for the maximum of aesthetic delight, therefore, Santayana discarded most of our aesthetic environment. And that is why his definition has not been accepted.

His own practice belies his definition in dozens of illustrations, and I would say in the connotations of every sentence he indites so rich with minor discriminations. When he observes that the pleasure in fine materials is keenest when these are presented in simple, unornamented extensions of surface, so that,

although the effect of extension is not that of material, the two are best seen in conjunction [and] very rich and beautiful materials do well to assume this form. [For] you will spoil the beauty you have by superimposing another; as if you make a statue of gold, or flute a jasper column, or bedeck a velvet cloak. . . . Even stone gives its specific quality best in great unbroken spaces of wall,[7]—

is he insisting on an objectification of pleasure in these materials? Very unlikely. Objectified or not, the sensuous enjoyment of the quality of materials is plainly a perception of their beauty. To insist on objectification would be arbitrary in the judgment of their value in perception. And so, throughout his book. His own evidence does not comport with his definition. The field of beauty in his own handling of it spreads out on all sides beyond the limits of his criterion of beauty. He follows the common sense test definition which he acknowledged at the beginning, and not his own explicit definition of objectified pleasure. That is, in spite of himself, the common sense test definition draws him out in his detailed descriptions beyond the limits of his deliberately chosen refined definition. I dwell on this point to exemplify the force of the common sense test definition in aesthetic analysis.

Logically Santayana might have stuck willfully to his definition of objectified pleasure, let the facts be what they might. It constitutes a natural boundary in the mechanistic mode of analysis. But it shuts out too much that is commonly regarded as aesthetic, too much even for Santayana to accept in his unguarded comments.

The next to the last field that Santayana described in his succession of exclusions is in my judgment the proper one for defining the aesthetic field in hedonistic terms—the field, namely, of immediate or intrinsic pleasures. I should also add intrinsic pains as negative aesthetic values. *Things liked or disliked for themselves* would thus be the field of aesthetic values *and the values would lie in the feelings of pleasure or displeasure.* This field is probably somewhat larger than the

[7] *The Sense of Beauty*, p. 100.

common sense test field, but there is no natural stopping place, in terms of the mechanistic categories, between Santayana's field and this one. Objectification is in the psychology of mechanism an actual psychological process to which feelings are susceptible. It is not an entirely arbitrary qualification, such, for instance, as pleasures recollected in moments of tranquillity would be. Of course, there is nothing oracular about a definition of aesthetic value as simply immediate pleasure or displeasure. It seems tame and commonplace. It also puts Beethoven in the same field with a culinary chef, and Titian with the painter of a pin-up girl. But is not that a good thing and to be counted as a merit of the hedonistic theory? Why should not Titian compete with the painter of a pin-up girl? For the rest, what is left out is qualities which no hedonic view can possibly present convincingly, the contributions of the other three approaches to the aesthetic field.

I recommend, accordingly, this unimposing definition instead of Santayana's. And it is, after all, a field Santayana himself recognized.

If, accordingly, aesthetic value is defined as feelings of immediate pleasure and displeasure, whence objects of aesthetic value are objects which produce or attract these feelings, then for the hedonic view this definition becomes the basic qualitative criterion of aesthetic judgment. What, we ask next, will be the relevant quantitative standards? These will be the intrinsic quantitative dimensions of pleasure and displeasure, namely, the number, duration, and intensity of them. Two pleasures are better than one, a longer pleasure than a shorter one, and an intenser pleasure than a weaker one, and conversely with displeasures as negative values. The more of immediate pleasure in an experience the greater the aesthetic value, and a great work of art is one that can be relied upon to produce a great deal of pleasure. This naked statement of the hedonic standard I am sure will seem gross, naïve, and revolting to some of you. Hedonistic writers on aesthetics usually cloak their standard more tactfully, and that may be one motive for qualifying the pleasure field in some way as Santayana did with "objectification."

But about such a reaction in opposition to the acceptance of an open statement of the hedonic standard in aesthetics, two comments may be made. The first is that the reaction is justified so far as it arises from a just sense that something is omitted in the strict hedonistic description of beauty. Yet in exoneration of the hedonist it should be added that what is omitted is something that no mechanistic account can convincingly present, since as lately mentioned it consists in the contributions of other world hypotheses to the subject.

The second comment is a warning to the high minded that unless pleasure in all its sensuousness, and closeness to the human body and bodily impulses is frankly recognized as the source of aesthetic judgment, vitality runs out of the field and the conception of aesthetic experience becomes dry or anemic. There is too little rather than too much emphasis on the contributions of the human body to aesthetic values, even among hedonistic writers. Even they tend to become over-refined, following out thin veinlets rather than the broad arteries of feeling. No, let us take our aesthetic pleasures straight. Let us accept them without a blush and for all they are worth.

So I give you the hedonistic standard boldly and as the frankly calculating thing that it is. For in fact pleasures do vary in intensity and duration and in fact they can in a manner be counted and compounded. There is more pleasure in a drink of cool water when you are thirsty than when you are not. And there is more pleasure for a hot and thirsty man to drink in the shade than to drink without the shade or than to sit in the shade without the drink. The difficulties in estimating amounts of pleasure are much exaggerated by non-hedonists. On the hedonic view, it is frankly the amount of immediate pleasure that gives the amount of aesthetic worth.

A number of consequences follow. I will spread these out as a series of steps leading up to the final one as regards the judgment of a work of art.

(1) First, since pleasures received from objects vary with the person and with his mood or physiological state, it follows that all elementary aesthetic judgments in the form "This gives me such an amount of immediate pleasure" are relative. The same object may give a different amount of pleasure, or even displeasure to another person or to the same person at another time. This is what Santayana refers to when he says, "It is unmeaning to say that what is beautiful to one man *ought* to be beautiful to another." [8]

From this consequence, people often jump to some false conclusions. One of these is that the hedonic judgment is not strictly speaking a judgment of fact but just a feeling and so paradoxically indubitable on the one hand, and irrelevant to truth on the other. Now, of course, a feeling is a fact, and, like any other fact so far as it is exactly what happened, it is not subject to doubt. But that does not signify that a man's cognition of it and report on it are not judgments subject to error like any other judgment. There is a widespread assumption that introspective reports, particularly if they refer to feeling or emotion, are not subject to error. This notion is abstractly possible, though it would have to be empirically demonstrated. That is, it would have to be shown by repeated observations that men never made errors in their introspective reports about their feelings. But in fact we know the reverse to be true, that men often deceive themselves about their own feelings. A girl may go to a party and be so disappointed at something that occurred that she will not admit her pain to herself and will come home and say as

[8] *The Sense of Beauty*, p. 41.

truthfully as she knows how that she had a good time. And even common sense is aware that people often attach their feelings to the wrong objects. A man will blow up his secretary because a business competitor outwitted him. But such illustrations to one side, the essential point is that an elementary aesthetic judgment in the form "I find immediate pleasure in this" is just like any other judgment. This is important because, being a judgment, it can if true or probable, be connected with other true or probable judgments to make a science. But indubitable feelings or preferences are often supposed to be immune to cognitive treatment and a science of aesthetics is thereby estopped, as also intelligent criticism.

A second conclusion jumped at from a recognition of the relativity of pleasures, and closely allied to the first, is that objective statements and general assertions about aesthetic matters must on account of the relativity be impossible. This conclusion is also absurd. As regards objective statements, every judgment supported by evidence of introspective report or external observation that "this gives immediate pleasure to so and so" is an objective statement. And as for general assertions, every work of art designed to appeal to a certain public is in the nature of a prediction that members of this public will derive immediate pleasure from that object. These predictions are verified often enough to provide a great mass of material for systematic general aesthetics. The bases of these generalizations are the essential biological similarity of human organisms, the similarity of their capacities for intellectual, emotional, and sensory development, and the similarity of reaction induced by identical cultural surroundings. From these similarities not only can the uniformities of reaction of individuals be fairly well anticipated, but also the differences. And what is more to the present issue, it is possible from these generalizations to point out the directions in which men can expect to find the greatest amount of immediate enjoyment. These directions consist in part in technical means of producing objects capable of rich and extensive delight, and in part of methods of cultivation by which men can increase their susceptibilities of enjoyment.

(2) This leads to the second consequence of the hedonistic definition of beauty, and that is the recognition that within the span of our life there are ways of increasing our capacities of enjoyment and there are places and objects in which these enjoyments are most fully to be found. This I think is what Pater means in the famous Conclusion of his *Renaissance:*

Every moment some form grows perfect in hand or face; some tone on the hills or the sea is choicer than the rest; some mood of passion or insight or intellectual excitement is irresistibly real and attractive to us,—for that moment only. Not the fruit of experience, but experience itself, is the end. A counted number of pulses only is given to us of a variegated, dramatic life. How may we see in them all that is to be seen in them by the finest senses? How shall we pass most swiftly from point to point, and be present always at the focus where the greatest number of vital forces unite in their purest energy?

It is unintelligent not to get the greatest pleasure out of life that life can give. In this we discover a certain obligation to ourselves, one that has its roots within ourselves. We ourselves would feel it a loss and would upbraid ourselves for our stupidity or inhibitions should we learn that great pleasures were within our reach which we did not take advantage of. Here then does enter a sense in which we do admit that we ought to enjoy what would give us the greatest enjoyment. Santayana is right in showing there is no sense in saying to a man who puckers his mouth at an olive, "You ought to like this olive." But he is unduly restricting the potentialities of his theory if he intends to deny the basis for the general advice, "You really ought to like olives, for it does not take long to overcome the dislike and there are so many occasions when one can enjoy olives." The application of this principle to aesthetic taste in general and to the fine arts is obvious.

A critic is, so to speak, a man who has learned to like olives. He is an expert in the ways of pleasures in special regions of experience. He may do a good deal of negative criticism with the purpose of helping the artist or warning the public. But his greatest service is constructive, in helping the public to get into pleasurable relation with objects of high capacity of enjoyment, showing them what to look for and encouraging them to become discriminating for themselves.

Several times I have said that the genius of hedonic criticism lies in its sensuous discrimination. The reason is that pleasures rarely or never come of themselves, but nearly always are embodied in some material and this is usually the sensuous material of sensations and images. To have pleasures in variety, and to avoid the risk of monotony, the hedonist seeks pleasures not directly but indirectly through the sensuous materials that embody them. He sees nature and a work of art through the sources of delight in sensation and images and consummations of form.

Here is an illustration: Santayana has just quoted the passage from *Saint Agnes' Eve* beginning:

> And still she slept in azure-lidded sleep,

and continues,

But the time may be near when . . . our poetry, with our other arts, will dwell nearer to the fountain-head of all inspiration. For if nothing not once in sense is to be found in the intellect, much less is such a thing to be found in the imagination. If the cedars of Lebanon did not spread a grateful shade, or the winds rustle through the maze of their branches, if Lebanon had never been beautiful to sense, it would not now be a fit or poetic subject of allusion. And the word "Fez" would be without imaginative value if no traveller had ever felt the intoxication of the torrid sun, the languors of oriental luxury, or, like the British soldier, cried amid the dreary moralities of his native land: —

> Take me somewhere east of Suez
>   Where the best is like the worst,
> Where there ain't no ten commandments
>   And a man may raise a thirst.

Nor would Samarcand be anything but for the mystery of the desert and the picturesqueness of caravans, nor would an argosy be poetic if the sea had no voices and no foam, the winds and oars no resistance, and the rudder and taut sheets no pull. From these real sensations imagination draws its life, and suggestion its power. The sweep of the fancy is itself also agreeable; but the superiority of the distant over the present is only due to the mass and variety of the pleasures that can be suggested, compared with the poverty of those that can at any time be felt.[9]

It dawns on me that there is a double appropriateness in Santayana's title "The *Sense* of Beauty." The second consequence of the hedonic standard of beauty, then, is the emergence of a general obligation to refine our senses so as to obtain the most pleasure of which our bodies are capable.

(3) Now, finally, the last consequence is that in view of the two previous consequences—namely, (1) that judgments of pleasure are objective, and (2) that there is an acknowledged internal obligation on the part of individuals so far as pleasures are concerned to have as much as they can get— it follows that the judgment of the value of a work of art in terms of its capacity to give immediate pleasure to individuals is also objective.

There is a strange perversity on the part of many hedonists which leads them to deny objectivity to their judgments of value. Actually the judgment of the capacity of a work of art to give pleasure is perfectly objective. When the relevant variables are put in, such as the degree of an individual's

---

[9] *The Sense of Beauty*, pp. 67–68.

hedonic discriminations and the influences of his cultural environment, the judgment is not only objective but stable and a sound basis for prediction. It is therefore possible to assert that a work of art of great aesthetic value is one that affords a great deal of immediate pleasure to a highly discriminatory taste. The only assumption is that an undiscriminating taste is at a disadvantage in its capacity of getting enjoyments from objects, which is a purely empirical matter open to verification. Whatever the state of discrimination which affords the intensest and most sustained delight in objects designed to give immediate pleasure, that degree of discrimination would endow its objects with the greatest aesthetic worth. The experience of most hedonic writers on aesthetics indicates that in any particular field of stimulation the maximum of discrimination yields the maximum of immediate pleasure. It follows that the aesthetic value of a work of art has nothing to do with the number of people who enjoy it, but only with the amount of enjoyment it gives to those people discriminating enough to enjoy it. The undiscriminating are missing something. Santayana expresses this principle when he writes, "Nothing has less to do with the real merit of a work of imagination than the capacity of all men to appreciate it; the true test is the degree and kind of satisfaction it can give to him who appreciates it most." [10]

If now it is asked, "How on this basis can a Titian be superior to a Varga girl?" the answer would be something like this: In the first place, any man who cannot appreciate a Varga girl is missing something. But, in the second place, a man who has not developed the discriminations to appreciate a Titian is missing something. The second man, moreover, assuming that he also appreciates a Varga, perceives that a Varga girl is little more than a paper substitute for a real girl who is much more worth appreciating than the pictures of

[10] *The Sense of Beauty*, p. 43.

her, whereas there is no substitute for a Titian. There really is more immediate pleasure in a Titian for any man of visually refined discriminations. That is why the hedonic critic recommends the cultivation of one's discriminations, and sets up the discriminating expert as the concrete embodiment of his hedonic standard.

3

Contextualistic Criticism

THE MECHANISTIC CRITICISM, you recall, springing as it does from a world hypothesis founded on the space-time field, lays great stress on the location of things. So, it locates a work of art as a physical object outside of an organism, and describes the path of stimulation from the physical object to the organism, and locates the value of the work among the responses of the organism in the form of pleasures correlated with these responses. The direct objects of aesthetic value, however, turn out to be sensations and images stimulated by the external object or associated with it. The human body and the boundaries of the body are accordingly prominent features in this type of criticism, for the values are conceived as centered in the body and confined within it.

When we turn to contextualism, all this is changed. The most striking feature of contextualism is the relative insignificance of the boundaries of the human body. The body becomes simply a constant detail in a man's changing environment somewhat like the clothes he wears and the profession he follows. The basic concept of contextualism is a context of activity. The word "situation" has recently been suggested for this idea by Otis Lee in an article entitled "Value and the Situation," [1] which is one of the clearest and most consistent statements yet to appear of this relatively new concept in philosophy. The concept of situations, he writes, "enables us

[1] *The Journal of Philosophy*, XLI (1944), 337–360.

to understand how values are objective, as common men believe them to be, and at the same time concrete, specific, and inherent in the process of . . . experience." [2]

By saying that "values are objective," he means precisely that they are not like a mechanist's conception of values confined to individual subjects, organisms, bodies, but are spread over a whole environmental situation.

A situation [he continues] includes both agents and circumstances, so action and the situation go together. The agent is faced by circumstances within the situation, and the act is his response to the problem they present. Through it the total situation, including both agent and circumstances, is changed in some way. There are three characteristics of the situation which make it important for the understanding of value: its unity, value potentialities, and problematic nature.

The situation is one. It is a natural fact with a natural unity, not a construct made and existing only in the mind. It is not an assemblage of people, things, events, qualities and relations, pleasures, pains, and interests, combined in and by the perspective of some given individual. All these are among its constituents, but it is itself an independent unit. Its unity is constituted by a characteristic quality, which is unique in each situation, though when we describe it we must use words which do or might apply to other situations as well—words such as cheerful, dynamic, hostile, peaceful, stimulating, competitive, and promising.

Language recognizes its existence. We say of people, "They found themselves in an unusual situation, which afforded exceptional opportunities," or, "His situation was desperate." We do not deal with the universe at large; neither do we deal with single things, events, or persons in succession. We are always acting within a limited setting which includes various circumstances, and probably other actors in addition to ourselves. In this sense the situation, including both agent or agents and the circumstances confronting him or them, is the unit of experience. Moreover, it has value quality, as is suggested by such descriptive words as those above: cheerful, dynamic, and hostile. [3]

[2] *Ibid.*, p. 337.
[3] *Ibid.*, pp. 338–339.

This description seems to come from another world than Santayana's. In a certain sense it does come from another world. It comes from a basically different way of handling the world's evidence, from a different world hypothesis. Contextualism is the youngest of the relatively adequate world views and is still in its tentative stages. But through the work of James and Peirce, Schiller and Bergson, Mead and Dewey, and many others it has already had a great influence on contemporary thought. It has produced operationalism in science, instrumentalism in logic, and a new kind of objective relativism in ethics and social theory. Its influence on aesthetic theory is equally pronounced, though I do not know by what name to call it other than contextualistic aesthetics.

Aesthetic experience is obviously to be found, on such a view, in a human situation. It has been uniformly identified, moreover, by competent contextualists with the qualitative side of a situation. As Otis Lee points out, every situation has its unique quality. There is pretty general agreement that the aesthetic character of a situation consists in the perception of its quality. Whether there should be any further qualification of the field depends on the question of its congruence with the field of the test common sense definition, referred to in the first lecture. And the field of humanly intuited qualities of events does seem too wide. Even when narrowed to vividly intuited quality, it includes toothaches and other involuntarily endured pains which common sense would never tolerate as positive aesthetic values. Accordingly, I suggest for the contextualistic definition of the aesthetic field: *voluntary vivid intuitions of quality*.

This appears to me a better definition than that of "enjoyable intuitions of quality" implied occasionally by contextualists, though it comes to much the same thing. Men will not voluntarily remain long in a painful experience. They turn it into a practical situation and seek means to get out of it.

A voluntary intuition of vivid quality is either pleasant or finds something so satisfying in the situation that it absorbs the pain. But if one wants to get at the particular force of contextualistic criticism, he does better not to think about the pleasure (leave that to the mechanist) but about the experience. The contextualist is a gourmand for experience. The stress is on the experience, the unique quality of the experience, and it is this that is quantified to give the contextualistic aesthetic standard. *The more vivid the experience and the more extensive and rich its quality, the greater its aesthetic value.* Whatever pleasure it contains is incidental, merely a contribution to the situation from an organism involved in it. As Otis Lee said, "pleasures, pains, and interests . . . are among its constituents, but it is itself an independent unit." Value lies in the situation as a whole, and the aesthetic value lies in the intensity and extensity of its quality. Irwin Edman in his *Arts and the Man* [4] states the view beautifully in these words,

Whatever experience may portend or signify, veil or reveal, it is irretrievably there. It may be intensified and heightened or dulled and obscured. It may remain brutal and dim and chaotic; it may become meaningful and clear and alive. For a moment in one aspect, for a lifetime in many, experience may achieve lucidity and vividness, intensity and depth. To effect such an intensification and clarification of experience is the province of art.[5]

Intensity and depth of experience—that is the contextualistic standard of beauty.

And let me say again that the evidential support for this definition of aesthetic value lies not alone in what it can do in the aesthetic field, but in its conformity with a mode of handling all evidence according to the contextualistic world

[4] *Arts and the Man; a short introduction to aesthetics* (New York: W. W. Norton & Co., 1939).
[5] *Ibid.*, p. 12.

hypothesis. Its success in the aesthetic field contributes to the evidence for the contextualistic world hypothesis, but the successes of this world hypothesis in other fields gives at the same time a wide corroborative support to the empirical justification of this definition.

Now I will expand some of the aesthetic implications of this view, and show their bearing on the judgment of a work of art. These may be brought out by a series of contrasts. I will arrange them in a pair of columns:

Quality	*vs.*	Relations
Intuition	*vs.*	Analysis
Fusion	*vs.*	Diffusion
Unity	*vs.*	Detail

The left hand column represents the aesthetic features of a situation; the right hand column, the analytical features which are for the most part the practical also. Every human situation has a certain proportion of both of these sets of features. For it is the quality that determines the unity and range of a situation (at least aesthetically) and it is the fused details and relations that determine the content. There is accordingly no sharp line in experience between the aesthetic and the non-aesthetic. Aesthetic value runs out into all life, though it runs pretty thinly through much of it. It is characteristic of contextualistic aesthetics that there is no negative aesthetic value. Beauty is found in a vivid realization of the quality of a situation, and, where vivid realization fails, beauty is absent. What we call ugliness, on this view, is a drab or painful situation calling for practical action, which we deplore because we feel morally that it ought to be beautiful. Ugliness is moral disapproval of the absence of aesthetic value in a situation. It is an ethical rather than an aesthetic evaluation. But this moral judgment is very close to the aesthetic. And it is another characteristic of contextualistic point of view not to admit of sharp lines between different spheres of judgment. So one is at a loss to say of Dewey's *Art as Experience*,[6] which has proved quite justifiably the most influential aesthetic work in contextualistic literature, whether it is mainly a book in aesthetics or in ethics. It is a crusade against all manner of attitudes and customs and social conditions which stand in the way of our getting the fullest realization of our environment and our lives.

But to return to our two columns of contrasted features of a situation. These will require explanation for anyone not familiar with them. Yet in a fundamental sense they defy explanation, since they are basic categories in this world hypothesis. They are ultimate concepts in terms of which other concepts are explained in contextualism. There is nothing one can do but point to them. So that is what I shall try to do by means of a stanza from a lyric of Coleridge's:

> A sunny shaft did I behold
> From sky to earth it slanted;
> And poised therein a bird so bold—
> Sweet bird, thou wert enchanted.
> —"Glycine's Song"

Now if you permit the image to form from this lyric and the words and the rhythm to have their way, something will surely have happened between you and these sounds in the brief time of my reading the verses. Whatever the quality of the previous moments in the context of this lecture room with the blackboard behind me and this desk in front and these seats and the listeners and the concepts of a theory being expounded, I am sure Coleridge's verses brought in an event with quite a different color. Well, that is what the contextualist means by quality. It is the character, the mood, and you might almost say, the personality of an event. You will

[6] John Dewey, *Art as Experience* (New York: Minton, Balch & Co., 1934).

not find it easy to give an adequately descriptive name to this stanza. "Cheerful," "optimistic," "anticipative"—these touch upon the quality of Coleridge's lines, but do not name it. It requires a proper name. That is what Otis Lee meant by speaking of a characteristic quality, "which is unique in each situation." If you wish to carry this principle of uniqueness to the limit, you will say that every one of us in the room had a different event with a different quality, and that for each one of us at another reading these verses will have yet another quality. As Dewey says, "A new poem is created by everyone who reads poetically. . . . Every individual brings with him . . . a way of seeing and feeling that in its inter-action with old material creates something new, something previously not existing in experience." [7] There is a truth in this insight never to be forgotten. There is an ultimate, irre-ducible relativity of contexts. Two situations never exactly repeat. It is the relativism of contextualism. But at the same time and by the same principle there is a connectedness of contexts, which is reflected in the qualities of the connected events. There is a family likeness among the qualities of my own separate readings of this poem, and without much ques-tion also among the qualities of your several simultaneous events in listening to it just now. So, it is possible to speak with a fairly high degree of approximation to agreement of *the* quality of the poem. We shall have more to say about this matter later; but for the present let it rest at this, that while technically it is true that the quality of every event is unique and unrepeated, practically the large amount of iden-tity of context in the perception of a work of art renders the differences relatively negligible, so that it is practically cor-rect to speak of an identical quality running through our technically different situations.

That, then, is what quality is. It is what you experienced

[7] *Art as Experience*, p. 108.

as the total character of the reading of those lines. Next observe that this character is derived from a fusion of the characters of the details interrelated within the stanza. Just single out the image of the bird poised in the shaft of light. That is a remarkably clear-cut unity. But see what goes to make it up. Observe some of the phrases and the words. Consider "sunny shaft" and "slanted" and "from sky to earth" (notice, not from earth to sky), and "I behold" just preceding "from sky" and suggesting looking up, and "poised therein," and "bold sweet bird," and "enchanted." It is an event magically, momentarily caught and crystallized and shaped into one unified image character. But on analysis we see that the character of the image grows out of a fusion, the cementing together or the interpenetration of the interrelated details.

Get the quality of "sunny shaft" by itself. Isolated as a separate event quoted out of its context, it has its own quality. And get the quality of "bold sweet bird." And then put them both back into their context in the total image, and do you not see that something has happened to them in their union in the total texture? That is their fusion. It is like the separate notes of a chord which fuse in the specific character of the chord, which yet is made out of the very characters of the notes that compose it. Fusion is thus pointed to as something ultimate, and unanalyzable, and immediate.

Now, let us see what all this comes to. Our little piece of analysis has succeeded in bringing out every term set down in the two contrasted columns. A situation or event is a unity with details. If we intuit the unity of it, as we did in the original reading, we get the quality of the event by a fusion of its interrelated details. If we analyze it to find the relations of its details, we diffuse the unity and lose the quality of the whole, or at least diminish its vividness in following out the details. Do you see that too? For we have done both. We have both synthesized and analyzed. We have had a first intuition of the total quality, and then we have partially analyzed the relations of the details which entered into it.

It must now be clear that the four terms in each column all go together, and amount to so many ways of designating either the wholeness or the composition of a situation.

It appears further that the two columns are correlative to each other. There is no such thing as a situation having a quality without interrelated details to make it up. And there is no such thing as an analysis of details unless there is a total situation to be analyzed into its details. Moreover, the two columns are inversely related: the greater the fusion and the intuition of the quality of the whole, the less the analytical sense of the separate details and their relations and vice versa. Moreover, there are all degrees of cognition from total fusion through the various proportions of intuition and analysis to complete analysis with just enough sense of the unity of the situation to give the analysis significance. Finally, vividness of quality is, with certain exceptions, associated with fusion and intuition, and loss of vividness with attention to relations and analysis.[8]

Of the four terms named in the first or aesthetic column,

[8] There seem to be two main exceptions: First, states of alertness, where in preparing to solve or meet a situation one is keenly observant of the details of the situation. In an emergency, for instance, perception is, for a man who keeps his head, very vivid and at the same time analytical. It is as though an organism could under conditions of emergency calling for exceptional output of energy be at once intuitive and analytical. The contrast between the two attitudes is here partially dissolved and we have almost the two in one, which suggests an ideal of perception congenial to organicism, the view coming up in the next lecture (cf. L. E. Hahn, *A Contextualistic Theory of Perception* [University of California Press, 1942], pp. 120–121).

The second exception is of an opposite nature, where through habit vividness is dulled though the fused intuition of the quality of the situation is undoubtedly there. This is the way we meet familiar objects about the town, familiar faces about the house.

But barring states of alertness and habit, then for all states of ordinary perception the correlation of vividness of quality with fusion, and of the loss of vividness in the quality of a total situation with analysis and diffusion seems to hold good.

fusion is the one likely to give most trouble and is, in a way, the key to the others. It is the process which connects the two columns by transmitting the separate details of the analytical situation into the unified quality of the aesthetic situation. It is ignored, disparaged, or explained away by most other world hypotheses—called merely subjective, a result of insufficient analysis, mere vagueness, or nothing but a lot of undiscriminated elements. In rebuttal the contextualist points to it as an ultimate categorial fact of immediacy. He insistently repeats that it cannot be explained away because it is something in terms of which he explains other things. And for that very reason it cannot be explained. One cannot explain an ultimate fact.[9]

[9] It is curious, by the way, how quickly the various modes of handling the aesthetic field bring us up against factual ultimates. In mechanism it was pleasure and pain and sense quality. In contextualism it is the fused quality of a total situation. It will be much the same with the coming views. Aesthetic issues are primarily over immediacies. In the aesthetic field more than anywhere else these issues over ultimate presented fact come to a head, and one has to learn how to deal with them. Immediate presentations cannot be thinned down to pointer readings, as in the physical field, and then all disagreements be turned over to what obviously have to do with interpretations of the readings. Aesthetic immediacies are full and rich and have to be met face on. When they conflict there are but two alternatives open: The first is arbitrarily to accept the deliverances of one kind of immediacy and to treat all the rest as the illusory results of conceptual bias. But this strikes me as utterly unwarranted in view of the other competing immediacies, and as clearly dogmatic. The second alternative is to treat them all as possibly influenced by conceptual interpretation, and to insist on corroboration in any case. This is the procedure of the present lectures, and is the reason for seeking the grounds of aesthetic criticism in the four relatively adequate world hypotheses. These hypotheses, in their descriptive content, are the empirical corroborations of the aesthetic immediacies they support; and in their conceptual structure, they account for the form these immediacies take, and give a clue to the degree of interpretation that may be involved.

In view of all this, more attention in the theory of knowledge could be profitably given to the aesthetic field than has been customary in the past. If the problem of knowledge is attacked exclusively from the field of the physical sciences or even from that of psychology with its rather slight present interest in aesthetic facts, the full impact of the issues over factual immediacy is not likely to be felt. Then a man comes to think there is no real issue over the facts but only over their interpretation.

But even if it cannot be explained, we can say things about it. For, of course, fusion is not explained by pointing out that the quality of a fusion is made up of the qualities of the details fused. The whole point about a fusion is that it results in a quality different from the qualities of any of its constituents. Once more I refer you back to Coleridge's lines read as a whole and our later analysis of its details. The quality of the fusion is different from the sum of the qualities of its analyzed factors. It is an emergent. Or to say the same thing in reverse and in a way that is perhaps more familiar, analysis always destroys something. It begins by destroying the vividness of the quality of the whole and may end by destroying the aesthetic whole.

Now, so far as the relevance of fusion to the aesthetic values is concerned, it is, I believe, equivalent to emotional perception. You remember William James identified emotion with the fusion (that was his own word) of organic and kinesthetic sensations. There is no very good reason why he should not have included the external sensations also when these are present. Actually, in any emotional reaction there is no clear separation of visual, auditory, or tactile sensations from the internal and dynamic ones. The sound of thunder is with difficulty distinguished from its fearfulness. The sound is fused with all the other things which W. B. Cannon shows enter into fear. Moreover, there are funded memories entering in. The fusion of all these makes up the specific fear of thunder. This basic insight of the James-Lange theory of emotion appears to hold in spite of all the criticisms of it. Only, what James should have stressed was not the kind of sensations that make an emotional quality, but the manner of their appearance, their fusion. In short, vividly fused experience is, for aesthetic purposes at least, a very convenient definition of emotional experience. When the fusion is massive and unmistakably draws in the dynamic tensions of instinctive action, no one would hesitate to call it emotional.

The importance of this comment is to suggest that the contextualistic account is the one that particularly takes care of the emotional aspect of aesthetic experience, and does so inconspicuously, realistically, and without the sentimentality and mythology of mysticism which parades its emotionality. It is symptomatic that Dewey frequently chooses the word "seizure" to designate the highest aesthetic experience. It is an experience in which a total situation is absorbed in a vivid fused satisfying quality.

How may vividness of quality be increased? This is best discovered by observing what produces its opposite. There are chiefly three causes for the reduction of vividness: (1) habit, convention, tradition, and the like; (2) practical activity in achieving goals; and (3) analysis.

Habit simply dulls experience and reduces it to routine. Practical activity ordinarily drains off vividness of quality by its urgency to attain its goal, or by producing a problem to solve which turns the attention away from the felt character of a situation to a solution in the future and escapes from the present. It also leads to analysis of the situation, in search for the means of solution, and the devivifying effect of analysis we have already brought out.

These then, one would think, should be scrupulously avoided in pursuit of aesthetic values. But one of the paradoxes of contextualism is that the last two, practical activity and analysis, when carefully applied, can be powerful agents for increasing quality. Human conflict, which is the greatest source of practical problems, is a potent means of intensifying experience by breaking up the dullness of routine, provided only the impulses involved can be held in contemplation and restrained from seeking practical solution. And analysis has a great capacity for increasing the spread of a vivid situation by exhibiting its structure and the details of its organization.

The ways in which artists have learned to increase the vividness of quality by the discreet use of conflict, and to increase the spread of quality by the organization of details, are known as the artists' techniques. The latter, the principles of composition, of design, pattern, and the intrinsic orders of sense materials are much better known to writers of aesthetics and criticism than the former—that is, the techniques of conflict. (Incidentally, notice how considerations of sense materials come up last in contextualistic aesthetics rather than first as in the mechanistic. The normal structure of a mechanistic book on aesthetics is from the elements to the wholes; that of a contextualistic book from the wholes to the details.) [10] It should not be said that the techniques of design and pattern are less important to the contextualistic critic than those of vivification through conflict, but certainly attention to the handling of conflict for aesthetic purposes is a peculiar contribution of contextualism.

It is remarkable how few contextualistic writers on art have noticed this. They tend to veer off after a good start in contextualism toward an integrative, organistic theory of art. If aesthetic value is a matter of vividness of quality, there is virtue in integration as a means of increasing the spread of quality through massive organization. This is an old story, the old story of harmonious unity. But it is something new in aesthetic theory to discover the aesthetic value of conflict. This side of his theory is what a contextualist should exploit. The integration he should stress is an integration of conflicts.

The techniques for the aesthetic use of conflict have been very little explored. The concept of "psychical distance" marks about the limit of it—that is, the idea that a man cannot get aesthetic value out of an experience that draws upon his emotions unless he can maintain an attitude that will keep these emotions from bolting into action. You can appreciate

[10] Compare, for instance, Santayana's *Sense of Beauty* with Pepper's *Aesthetic Quality*.

a storm as long as you are not prompted to look for a lifeboat, and you can appreciate Hamlet as long as he does not remind you too much of your own personality problems. That is about as far as criticism along these lines has gone. But very few have noticed the reverse of this idea, which is much the more interesting, that in proportion as these conflicts do touch you (to the point of not precipitating action) the aesthetic value of the experience is increased.

This fact has two important aesthetic bearings. For one thing, it explains in large degree the force of tragedy in art. Most of what we have taken to be our greatest art is outright tragedy or contains tragic portions. To a hedonist this is a mystery. Why in the temple of pleasure do we set up a god of sorrow? A contextualist explains that when the center of aesthetic interest is placed on vivid realization of experience, then the attraction of the artist to tragic subject matter is seen as inevitable. Conflicts of instinctive impulse and social interest stir our awareness of experience to the deepest, and the further they can be carried in a work of art towards their full tragic import the more vivid our realization. Tragedy in art then becomes no paradox.

The second bearing of the use of conflict in art is ethical. We now begin to understand how moral values enter into art. For in spite of the hedonists' efforts like that of the early Santayana to separate morality from art as something purely negative, or, like that of Pater to seek to identify moral and aesthetic values, we recoil and feel that the relation is not so simple. The conviction persists that the ethical values are different from the aesthetic, and that nevertheless in the most serious art they somehow get intimately involved with each other. Now we see that this is indeed the case, and why it happens. An artist seeks out social issues because they reflect conflicts and are sources of vivid realization of experience. In this way, an artist becomes a more powerful moral influence than a social reformer. For he possesses the techniques for making us vividly aware of our problems and cultivates a keenness of perception for precisely what are the sources of human conflict. Think how many essays were written with mild effect about the farm labor problem in America until Steinbeck came out with *The Grapes of Wrath*. Then for the first time the problem became vivid through the technique of an artist.

Dewey's prevailing message that art should get closer to living and that it grows weak when it is taken as luxury and entertainment and separated from the main stream of practical everyday contemporary living, is contextualistically sound. And a corollary of this principle is that art is perennially contemporary. So far as art depends on culture and not upon instinct, the art of one age cannot be vividly repeated in another, and, if the art of an earlier age appeals to a later, it is often for other than the original reasons, so that as contextualists repeat, sometimes too insistently, critics are required in each age to register the aesthetic judgments of that age.

We can already see what is expected of the critic on the contextualistic view. He is to judge the degree of realization of experience achieved by an artist—the vividness and the spread of it. He will consider whether the artist has made the most of his emotional material, or has gone beyond the limits of aesthetic endurance and destroyed aesthetic distance. He will show the relation of the work to its social context. He will consider the suitability of the structure of the work. And for the benefit of the spectator he will analyze the structure and exhibit its details, so that these will not be missed and may be funded in the full realization of the work in its total fused quality.

So much we see of what the critic is expected to do. But we have not yet seen what a work of art is on this view. And until we have, we cannot entirely comprehend the critic's rôle. For the description of the nature of a work of art furnished by a consistent application of the contextualistic approach is one of the special contributions of this theory. With that description and its bearing on criticism, I shall conclude this lecture.

The perception of a work of art is clearly the awareness of the quality of a situation. There are obviously two main factors in the situation of perceiving a work of art, and it is the relation of these two factors through successive perceptions of the identical work that is to be noticed. I think I can make this situation, or rather the succession of situations, clearer by a diagram. The two main factors are first, what we ordinarily call the physical work of art—that is, the stone or bronze of a statue, the canvas and pigments of painting, the score of a piece of music, the paper and print of a book—and, second, the spectator. Here is the diagram:

Physical Work of Art

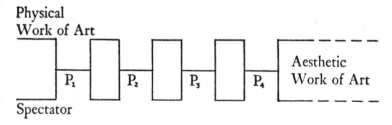

until we have, we cannot entirely comprehend the critic's

The upper line represents the physical work of art, the lower line the spectator. If you follow these along, you will see they are both continuous lines. When they come together at P_1, P_2, P_3 . . . we have perceptual situations. Suppose we think of a picture, say El Greco's "Toledo" in the Metropolitan Museum. The physical picture has had a long continuous history since El Greco laid the pigments on the canvas. And, supposing I am the spectator, so have I as an organism and personality had a long continuous history—

though not so long. When I first saw the "Toledo," that was P_1. Some time later I saw it again, P_2, and so on. And I hope to see it yet many times to come, which is the meaning of the dotted lines.

Now whatever the nature of the physical work of art apart from the spectator, we know it has not the quality of the perceived picture, for the quality of the perception includes colors and line movements and clouds and hills and city walls and these require the action of a spectator in the situation before they can appear. Similarly the quality of that El Greco did not exist for the spectator, for me, till I first came in contact with the physical picture in the Metropolitan Museum. The quality of the "Toledo," then, arises out of a situation to which the physical work of art and the spectator are both contributing. It requires the two in contact to produce the perception and realize the quality. It is true that the spectator can, once he has perceived the picture, bring up the memory of it, but we shall not here concern ourselves with this phase of the matter nor with photographs or other possible reproductions of the original. Strictly speaking, the quality of the picture is only realized on the occasions when it is actually perceived. Each such experience is an aesthetic experience.

But the next point is the important one. Normally each successive perception funds the previous one and adds something new not perceived before. Some new detail comes out, some line carries through as not observed before, some shape is seen as a contrast or subtle variation of another. These potentialities were in the picture from the beginning, but now for the first time I see them. And so the picture increases in breadth and vividness of quality from perception to perception. Not that there is a steady increase. Sometimes I am fatigued and see and feel it less than at earlier times. And sometimes I analyze it and voluntarily reduce quality for that perception in order to fund the results of the analysis in future perceptions and so increase the quality. But in general and over a number of perceptions, the realization of the work increases.

What all this means is that the aesthetic work of art is the cumulative succession of intermittent perceptions. It is $P_1 + P_2 + P_3 + \ldots$. The aesthetic work of art is not continuous but intermittent. This fact has rarely been given sufficient attention. But the intermittency and fugitive nature of the aesthetic work of art does not stand in the way of a high degree of objectivity in the aesthetic judgment of it. For the potentiality of the cumulative series of perceptions and of the ideal of the fully realized and funded perception at the end of the series lies in the actual continuity of the physical work of art. It lies in this and in the continuity of each spectator and in the considerable degree of uniformity in the perceptive capacities of different spectators.

The only adequate judgment of a work of art, therefore, is one based on the fullest realization of it, on a perception which contains the funded experiences of many preceding perceptions. An initial perception is superficial and untrustworthy unless the spectator has had much experience with similar works, or unless the work is clearly very simple and requires no further experience. Moreover, any one man's judgment of a very rich work of art is likely to need supplementation from that of another. For every spectator has his blind spots, and, to reach a complete judgment of a work of art, many men are needed in order to draw out its total capacity of realization. A complete aesthetic work of art thus becomes an ideal, realizable in the lesser works but perhaps rarely fully realized in the greater—possibly not even by the creating artist himself so many possibilities of realization may unconsciously enter in. It is that ideal final perception which rolls up all that is relevant in the line of preceding perceptions and intuits the whole potentiality of the physical work of art in a total vivid seizure.

This conception of the aesthetic work of art as a succession of cumulative perceptions leading up to a total funded perception which realizes the full appreciative capacities of the physical object seems to me the soundest and most fruitful to have appeared. It can be adapted to other points of view in aesthetics, but it generates spontaneously only out of the contextualistic.

Ironically, the contextualist himself does not seem to be able to make the most of it. He is so impressed with evidences of historical change and cultural influences and the shifting contexts of value that he cannot easily bring himself to accept any degree of permanence in aesthetic values. I would be far from asserting that beauty is eternal. But on the evidence of the other three world hypotheses I am convinced that there is much more permanence in the world than the contextualist admits. And I believe that the capacity of a great work of art to be appreciated exists as long as the physical work exists and there are men to perceive it. So far as a work of art appeals to our common instincts and our deepest emotions, it can move men of whatever age or culture. It may from accident of language and fashion and national or religious bigotry come in and out of popularity, but there it is ready to move the common man or the student who will put himself in contact with it. Potentially, the contextualist has given us an empirical basis for this belief.

But even if the contextualist does not care to take full advantage of his discovery, he has uncovered a new function for the critic. That is to contribute as far as he can to the complete realization of great works of art. The critic acquires a sort of creative function. It is something more than giving an expert judgment on the aesthetic value of the work. It is an act of producing the values latent therein. And it requires the co-

operation of many perceptive men to do this, since the capacities of a great work of art for aesthetic appreciation can
rarely be compassed by one man alone. Many men contribute
their perceptions and gradually the full potential perception
comes to light. When this is achieved, the aesthetic work of
art has attained its final judgment.

If the contextualist himself displays a skepticism about
final judgments of any kind, we will respect his testimony, but
we will balance it against that of other men of equal compe-
tence in handling the evidence. To one of these we shall turn
in the next lecture.

4

Organistic Criticism

ORGANICISM, traditionally known as objective idealism, is the world hypothesis that stresses the internal relatedness or coherence of things. It is impressed with the manner in which observations at first apparently unconnected turn out to be closely related, and with the fact that as knowledge progresses it becomes more systematized. It conceives the value of our knowledge as proportional to the degree of integration it has attained, and comes to identify value with integration in all spheres. Value in the sphere of knowledge is integration of judgments; in the sphere of ethics, it is integration of acts; in the sphere of art, it is integration of feelings. Finally, it conceives all of these as contained in a total integration of existence or reality.

Like contextualism, it is not impressed with the apparent boundaries of men's bodies. It deals with situations, but regards a contextualistic situation as merely a way station to a larger integration. It speaks of anything short of total integration as a fragment—meaning literally a fragment of the whole to which it ultimately and really belongs. By "really belongs," it means that when we have come to understand or achieve the whole of which the fragment was a part, we will recognize that the fragment was all along an integral part of that whole and that the apparent separateness of the part was merely due to our failure to perceive it in its relations to the other parts in the whole. It was due, as the organicist is fond of saying, to "the weakness of the spectator."

Now, we need not concern ourselves with the question of the final adequacy of this view of things. It is clear even from the few references I have made that it receives a great deal of corroboration. In the field of aesthetic appreciation and criticism it has proved to be possibly the most fruitful of all views. Schelling was the first to bring out the full extent of its implications, but Coleridge with the sensitiveness of a poet should probably be credited with the discovery of its powers as an instrument of criticism. Hegel rolled it ponderously over the whole field of cultural history in art, and is perhaps largely responsible for the intense modern interest in that subject. But most of his followers in aesthetic theory seem to me to have been more absorbed in developing the permutations of its concepts than in following its guidance among aesthetic facts, until finally Bosanquet gathered together the scattered results of a century of organistic thought and in his brief *Three Lectures on Aesthetic* [1] brought out one of the masterpieces in the literature of aesthetics. In its honesty, and modesty, and simple-minded consistency, and earnestness in keeping the reader in constant touch with the facts, it is not likely to be surpassed by any future exponent of the view. It is the more remarkable in that Bosanquet obviously lacks aesthetic sensitivity of the sort which emanates from every sentence that Coleridge writes. But he has the thing which Coleridge lacks, the perseverance to carry an idea through. If Bosanquet and Coleridge could be combined, the one for his intuitive grasp of the theory in its concrete workings and the other for his theoretical insight into its aesthetic meanings, we should have the perfect writer of organistic aesthetics and criticism.

I should like to introduce you to the view through Bosanquet's *Three Lectures*. Soon after the opening he gives a

[1] Bernard Bosanquet, *Three Lectures on Aesthetic* (London: Macmillan & Co., 1931).

succinct statement of the fundamental principle of organicism. "I only know in philosophy," he says, "one method; and that is to expand *all* relevant facts, taken together, into ideas which approve themselves to thought as exhaustive and self-consistent." [2] I cannot stop to comment on this condensed statement which is the mature fruit of a century of thought on the method of this world hypothesis. But I would have you note, for this point often escapes critics of organicism, that the self-consistency of which he speaks is not the mathematical self-consistency of abstract symbols. It is the self-consistency of "*all* the relevant facts." It is the coherence, the integrated connectedness, of *facts*. Bosanquet is enunciating a material principle. The kind of self-consistency he is pointing out is one that can be found only by following the guidance and the compulsion of the facts.

He proceeds to apply this principle to the aesthetic field. He first says something that sounds a good deal like unqualified hedonism. "The simplest aesthetic experience," he writes, "is a pleasant feeling, or a feeling of something pleasant—when we attend to it, it begins to be the latter." The stress, however, is on the "*something* pleasant." He goes on, "It is a *relevant* feeling—I mean it is attached, annexed, to the quality of some object—to all its detail." Stopping now, we might think this was Santayana's objectified pleasure. But next, "My feeling in its special quality is evoked by the special quality of the something of which it is the feeling, and in fact is one with it." [3] Now the feeling begins to take on a contextualistic tone, the "quality" of the experience, "in all its detail," is what comes out. Moreover, the feeling quality presently passes out of the individual into the situation in which many individuals share. "The aesthetic attitude," he presently writes, "is that in which we have a feeling which is so embodied in

[2] Page 3.
[3] Pages 3 to 5.

the object that it will stand still to be looked at, and, in principle, to be looked at by everybody." [4] But one senses as he proceeds that the emphasis in his treatment of the aesthetic situation is being shifted off the quality stressed in the contextualistic treatment to something else. Finally, Bosanquet comes to the definitive point.

Feeling becomes "organised," "plastic," or "incarnate" [he writes]. This character of Aesthetic feeling is all-important. For feeling which has found its incarnation or taken plastic shape cannot remain the passing reaction of a single "body-and-mind." . . . Say you are glad or sorry at something. In common life your sorrow is a more or less dull pain, and its object—what it is about —remains a thought associated with it. There is too apt to be no gain, no advance, no new depth of experience promoted by the connection. But if you have the power to draw out or give imaginative shape to the object and material of your sorrowful experience, then it *must* undergo a transformation. *The feeling is submitted to the laws of an object.* It must take on permanence, order, harmony, meaning, in short value. [5]

Do you see that now we have passed quite beyond pleasure? We are talking about an embodiment of sorrow. And do you see also that it is not the quality of the experience that Bosanquet stresses but its organization or embodiment? To reach the organistic idea, one is not far off if he starts with the vivid situation of the contextualist and instead of stressing the quality and defining the unity of the situation by the quality, stresses the organization and defines the unity of the situation in terms of its organization. Though it is not entirely satisfactory because of the ambiguity of the word "feeling," we probably cannot do better than accept the usual expression of the organistic definition of aesthetic value as the *integration of feeling.*

By "feeling" must be carefully understood the qualitative

[4] Page 6.
[5] Pages 7, 8.

side of experience in contrast with the practical and the logical; something more than the pleasant and painful. The organicist is not much concerned about defining feeling precisely, because in the higher integrations it merges with the ethical and logical connections anyway, and in the simpler pleasant or painful experiences it is obviously distinct from practical activity or logical judgment. Incidentally, painful experiences are intrinsically disintegrative, so that pains get absorbed or sifted out inevitably in the progress of integration. The aesthetic field is really defined by its origins among pleasures and the kind of connections indigenous to these origins rather than by any special sort of subject matter.

If you ask an organicist what these feeling connections are, he will ask you in effect if you have not felt the demand of pleasant things for other pleasant things to complete them or fill them out. Have you never been a bit of a creative artist in planting a garden, arranging flowers, putting a room in order, hanging up tools in the basement, making a speech, or even just carrying on a conversation? Do not gaps appear that ask to be filled in certain ways—ways that practically or logically are not called for, but that just make you feel better when they are followed out? There is no practical reason why you should put magazines in two piles on either side of the lamp on the parlor table, and as the logicians have been telling everybody there is certainly no logical reason for it since any arrangement is an order. But the magazines feel better that way. We say the two piles balance each other, and the lamp in the middle seems to ask for them too. Well, that is a feeling connection.

If you are walking alone down the front path, ten to one you walk down the middle of it. That is a series of feeling connections. When you selected your tie this morning did not you think a bit about the color of your suit and shirt and possibly also whether later in the day you were going to a reunion of old pals or to a tea party on Garden Street? That was a whole texture of feeling connections. If these connections are felt out with care, they will be found different for every situation. It takes imagination, we say, to feel them out. And here we come upon the organicist's special use of the term "imagination." It was, I believe, Coleridge who first called this activity the "creative imagination." It is the process of following out and building up feeling connections. With this in mind, another definition of aesthetic value for an organicist could be "imaginative integration."

There are two quantitative dimensions that yield organistic standards of beauty—the degree of integration and the amount of material integrated. By degree of integration is meant the thoroughness with which feeling connections are carried out in an aesthetic object. The maximum of integration is a condition where every detail of the object calls for every other and no feeling demands are unfulfilled. Or negatively, it is a condition where no detail can be removed or altered without marring or even destroying the value of the whole. Such a whole is called an organic unity, whence the name organicism. The degree of organicity is the intensive dimension of value in this theory.

The amount of material taken up into the organic whole is the extensive criterion. This standard may be a little deceptive, for the size or length of a work may not be indicative. A woven Indian basket may have more aesthetic material taken up in it than the Eiffel Tower. Aesthetic material is not just what the eye and the ear respond to but also the images and meanings and emotions below the sensory surface. Anything that begets a feeling connection is aesthetic material. And ultimately there is probably nothing that may not be drawn into an aesthetic integration. Politics and business, medicine, factory labor, collecting tickets, working on the railroad, and obviously war and religion have often been aesthetically em-

bodied. A work of art that embodies a massive reference to
these things is a large work though it be only fourteen lines
long.

> Late and soon,
> Getting and spending we lay waste our powers,

and the rest of this sonnet is a big work. A view of our civilization and an ethical judgment is aesthetically embodied here.

Just how much bigger one aesthetic object is than another
cannot be measured with scales and a ruler. Since there is no
urgent practical reason why we should ever want to know to
a unit and decimals the relative aesthetic sizes of two objects,
I doubt if we shall seriously try to improve on an experienced
man's judgment in such matters. There is, after all, no more
difficulty in judging that *Macbeth* is much bigger than
Anthony Adverse just in the amount of aesthetic material incorporated than in seeing with the eye that a full grown oak
is bigger than a birch sapling. Nevertheless, though physical
size is not an indication of aesthetic bigness, it does take a good
deal of physical size to incorporate a very large amount of
aesthetic material. Most of the works we think of as the
greatest are also physically pretty big. The greatest fiction
is among novels rather than short stories; the greatest poetry
is among epics and dramas rather than sonnets; the greatest
pictures are among oils, temperas, and frescoes rather than
miniatures; the greatest architecture among tombs, temples,
and cathedrals rather than domestic houses. Bigness is aesthetically important and to obtain aesthetic bigness a certain amount
of physical bigness is likely to be necessary.

As between a highly integrated jewel box, however, and a
poorly integrated cathedral with a lot of scattered charm,
which is the better? When degree of organicity and amount
of aesthetic material vary inversely, how does one adjudicate
between the standards? I think the organicist would not try

to adjudicate. You already have the aesthetic judgment when you have seen that the one object has aesthetically utilized its small amount of aesthetic material to the greatest advantage, and the other has failed to make the most of the large amount of positive aesthetic values that it has. Why ask for anything more?

I think you must by now have got something of the spirit of the organistic theory of beauty. Let me next draw some of its aesthetic consequences. I shall select three—its conception of the objectivity of aesthetic judgment, its theory of aesthetic criticism, and its interpretation of ugliness.

Organicism proposes a justification for a final objective judgment for a highly integrated work of art. Notice the limitation of objectivity to the integrated work. The point is that, in consistency with the general organistic concept of objectivity as identical with organicity, it would follow that objectivity of judgment can only arise in the apprehension of a high degree of organicity of fact. The organistic critic is, therefore, very secure in his positive judgments of the beauty of a highly organized work of art, but his negative judgments regarding the degree of failure of a rather unintegrated work would, he admits, be erratic and subjective, since he has very little to get a purchase on.

All of us must have had the experience of being asked to give a judgment of an immature or mediocre work. The difficulty is likely to be in finding anything specific to say. It is just generally not very good. There are no clues as to any particular way of pulling the thing together. Nothing calls particularly for anything else. Or, saying the same thing the other way around, there are so many ways in which some one little group of materials in the work might have developed in the hands of a man who felt their potentialities, that to explain to the maker of the object what he might have done with these materials would be virtually constructing a whole new work of art for him. For nothing else in the work confirms these particular potentialities. Moreover, you could just as well have taken another little group of materials from another part of the work and done the same thing with them, virtually constructing a totally different organization for him. The potentialities of the materials have nowhere been carried through and there are a bewildering number of conflicting potentialities of different materials. After looking over the work a while, you probably resort to asking him what he was trying to do.

Now, there is a rather widespread conception that this is the question one should always ask an artist before beginning to criticize his work. In fairness to the artist, it is said, you should not criticize him for not doing something he was not trying to do. So, you want to know first what he was trying to do, and then you will judge if he did it. This is good advice to inexperienced persons or to critics who are caught in a rut and need some assistance to get out. It calls attention to the possible weakness of the spectator. But if the spectator is not weak, there is no reason why the work of art should not explain itself. It can only obtain objectivity of judgment if it does, and, if it is thoroughly integrated, it both explains itself and has an objectivity of value.

So, if you are a man experienced in the potentialities of the materials of an art, and ask the artist what he was trying to do, it amounts to saying that whatever it was he was trying to do he did not succeed in doing it. What you are hoping is that he may have had an idea but lacked the ability to develop it, for then you can give him some assistance perhaps as to what materials to follow through and as to where he failed to answer demands of his materials and the like. When it is necessary to ask an artist what he was trying to do, either the spectator or the artist is weak. It is a question that an honest critic should never be afraid to ask, and that a critic secure in experience would be sure to ask when puzzled, for the most experienced critic has always something to learn about the potentialities of his art. But the question is intrinsically entirely irrelevant to the judgment of the aesthetic worth of an object. The aesthetic value of a work of art as an integration of feeling is as independent of any artist's subjective idea of what he wanted to do when he was making it, as the cognitive value of a scientific description of fact is independent of a scientist's idea of what he wanted to find when he started observing.

In the hands of a competent artist a work of art makes itself, so to speak, and the further it gets along the more nearly it does so literally. There are many anecdotes of novelists who found their characters taking the development of the story over into their own hands. The constant testimony of the force of inspiration points to the same thing. The aesthetic materials seek their own satisfying structure and equilibrium through the artist, who does not dictate but follows their guidance.

The organicist's view of artistic creation is thus part of his conception of the objectivity of the aesthetic work of art and of the judgment of it. Artistic creation is the creative imagination at work, and this consists in following through faithfully the demands of feeling in aesthetic materials, bringing into the work materials called for by other materials till a complete organic unity is established. Then the work stops of itself, is self-explanatory, and objective.

At the earlier stages of artistic creation a fragment of material has many alternative completions and is indeterminate. "Shaft" by itself is indecisive. It might be part of a carriage. It might be hundreds of metaphorical things. Any decision about its meaning would be arbitrary and subjective. But "sunny shaft" converts it suddenly into a thing. Now it is part of a definite whole and is controlled by "sunny" so as not to become part of a wagon, and "sunny" in turn is controlled by "shaft" so as not to become a male part of a family.

But "sunny shaft" has its own range of indeterminacy and might enter many wholes. If we follow the feeling tensions of it, not the logical, to reach an imaginative whole in which it would find companionship, "sweet bird, enchanted" feels immensely right. And now "sunny shaft . . . sweet bird enchanted" leads to "poised therein" and "I behold" and then inevitably "from sky to earth it slanted." There has been a mood all through this construction gaining in precision. It may have vaguely preceded the whole thing, and gathered up "sunny shaft," "bird," and "enchanted" by affinity. But now partially embodied in these images it acquires shape itself and naturally begins to dance to itself, Ta-túm-ta-tá-ta-túm-ti-tó ta-túm-ti-tú-ti-tá-ta. The words and images already in the mood enter into the dance, and distribute themselves in time, and, through the vowel sounds and consonants of the words, modify and specify the indeterminate little rhythm, and presently all these fragments come out together in the integrated stanza:

> A sunny shaft did I behold
>   From sky to earth it slanted
> And poised therein a bird so bold—
>   Sweet bird, thou wert enchanted!

Looking back, we shall see a lot of other feeling connections, altogether too many to catalogue. We see, for instance, how right "behold" was in relation to the embodied mood—to "enchanted," for instance. "I beheld" is not as magical and romantic as "I did behold." So, the "did" was functional and not a syllable to fill a beat in the verse. Moreover, the long $\bar{o}$ of "behold" is a tone the whole stanza longs for. It almost justifies "so bold" merely for its sound. In fact, it does. "A bird so bold" which in a juvenile rhymster would make you wince at the inversion for the sake of a rhyme not yielded by "so bold a bird," here gets a justification because that tone is needed in that place prominently, and the inversion landing the tone on the rhyme gives it a prominence that more than doubles its value. It is further weighted by the assonance of "so" just before it and the alliteration of the "b" in "bird," which binds the "bold" significantly back to the "bird." And there is a premonition of all this in the word "poised" at the beginning of the line, for "p" is allied to "b" and "oi" to "ō." The inversion, moreover, is slightly archaic and goes with "enchanted" and "did." What would *as a rule* be a defect becomes functional in the integrated embodiment of this feeling. Nor have we yet finished with the word, for it stands out in a way like a question, and the answer is in the rest of the poem beyond the first stanza. It might be called the very theme of the poem, or, to use a Victorian term, its moral. For doesn't the poem say subtly, "It's spring, be bold"?

Now think of the stanza again. Would not you know it was a fragment even if I had not told you, or you had not known there were other stanzas? When quoted in the last lecture, did it not feel incomplete in spite of the complete clarity of the image? Now, here is the rest of the poem. The same kind of imaginative construction we have done for the first stanza, following out the feeling connections of the materials, can be carried right on, and when the poem is finished, I ask you if there is not a rounded completeness about it, and if the first lines and the last and all the lines between do not coöperate with one another to make that completeness, and I ask further if there is a phrase or even a word taken in its context that could be changed without loss to the whole?

GLYCINE'S SONG

A sunny shaft did I behold,
From sky to earth it slanted:
And poised therein a bird so bold—
Sweet bird, thou wert enchanted!

> He sank, he rose, he twinkled, he troll'd
>   Within that shaft of sunny mist;
> His eyes of fire, his beak of gold,
>   All else of amethyst!
>
> And thus he sang: "Adieu! adieu!
> Love's dreams prove seldom true.
> The blossoms, they make no delay:
> The sparkling dew-drops will not stay.
>   Sweet month of May,
>   We must away;
>   Far, far away!
>   To-day! to-day!"

This I offer as a rough illustration of the way of the creative imagination. I do not say that this is how Coleridge came into the construction of his poem. One of the characteristics of an organic whole is that, however you come into it, you will reach the same result in the end because every detail is organically related to every other. Had he started from the second stanza or the last, he would have come out the same. Ask yourself what could in emotional congruence have sung the song of the last stanza except a bird so bold, or a fairy, and, of course, the bird was a fairy and in the mood of the song is not the fairy better in the form of the bird?

Now I am not sure that all of you will agree with all of the comments I have made on this poem. But if you follow the way of the creative imagination in a highly integrated poem like this, I am assured that you and I could come to a large amount of agreement about it, and I would be as likely to change my attitude in the light of your comments as perhaps you in the light of mine. For the point is that the materials of this poem are highly controlled in their interrelations, so that there is a constant test of relevancy within the work itself. It can be profitably discussed and constructed or reconstructed. This internal control is what is meant, according to the insight of the organicist, by the objectivity of a work of art. And now I think it must be clear why only highly integrated embodiments of feeling have this objectivity.[6]

This objectivity of a work of art and accordingly of the aesthetic judgment of it was, you recall, the first of three consequences we were going to trace resulting from the organistic definition and standards of aesthetic value. We now come to the organistic theory of criticism. This follows immediately from the organistic conception of aesthetic objectivity, and is, to my mind, one of the most fruitful contributions of any philosophy to aesthetic theory.

The idea is that the critic recreates in the process of judgment what the artist creates. In fact, I should expand the range

[6] We have in this process of the creative imagination the explanation of that paradox in the aesthetic experience noted by Kant in one of the antinomies of the *Critique of Judgement*—the sense of purposiveness without a purpose. Lately Bertram Morris in his *Aesthetic Process* (Evanston: Northwestern University, 1943) has made this the central theme of his analysis. He makes a reference to Kant (footnote, p. 77) which is a happy one and rather forgotten by most writers in this connection, and then summarizes his thesis in these sentences: "We have distinguished between art as the unfolding aesthetic process, and beauty as the completed experience. The two tend to coalesce . . . between fulfilling and fulfilment. . . . Purpose is [here] nothing more or less than purposiveness realized; but we must not confuse the aesthetic purpose with a set purpose which is intellectually anticipated in advance of, and apart from, the sensuous material. . . . [Aesthetic] purpose is not cold, meticulous intellect at work, but is that which completes experience and satisfies the imagination. The relations within this complex have no loose ends, which would thwart perception. Purpose may not be abstracted as something separate from the art-process; it is precisely the end of the process as cumulative resolution" (p. 78). This is not a bad way of describing the process, for it lies midway between practical conation and that sort of passive or receptive sensuousness characteristic of the hedonistic aesthetic and not entirely escaped in the intuited quality of the contextualistic aesthetic. A hostile writer is likely to pose the dilemma: either explicit practical purpose with a definite conceptual goal aimed at and attained, or passive receptivity of enjoyment without a goal. The Kantian antinomy and Morris's paradox of an aesthetic purpose that is not a set purpose, break the dilemma open and strikingly exhibit this third sort of mental being which is neither conation nor sensation but a specific aesthetic activity. Morris's name for it is "the satisfied imagination," which is a good phrase if "satisfaction" does not connote *hedonic* satisfaction too strongly.

of application of this recreative process, for it is not only the critic but any appreciative spectator who is expected to do this. There is no essential difference between criticism on this view and the process of attaining a full appreciation of aesthetic values on the part of any spectator. An understanding spectator is a critic, and a critic is simply an understanding spectator who is perhaps a little more articulate in communicating the experiences he has in a work of art. Everyone is expected to be active in his relations with a work of art. For how else can one sense the tensions, and connections, demands, fulfillments, satisfactions, and consummation in an organic integration of the aesthetic materials, unless one actively enters into them and feels with them as the artist did?

Even the difference between artist and spectator is partially broken down on this view. Both actively enter into the feeling tensions of the materials, both imaginatively work these up toward an organic structure for the satisfaction of all elements in a total mutual fulfillment. The only difference is that the artist had to bring the materials together and construct a whole that did not actually exist before, while a spectator may follow the guidance of the artist. The artist creates, the spectator recreates.

Now the way criticism comes in is like this: As the spectator imaginatively follows the feeling demands of the materials, sensing their potentialities, acknowledging and delighting in their fulfillments here, here, and here, becoming more and more excited as the organic structure begins to close in and the consummation comes in sight, he is perhaps suddenly blocked in one of his expectations. Here at this point the artist went one way where the spectator would have gone another.

Such a blockage is an automatic negative judgment on the part of the spectator. And notice how specific it is. An organistic critic makes no vague sweeping disapprovals. He is able to say precisely what is wrong for him and why. In his imaginative reconstruction he is frustrated at this point in expectations aroused by such and such and such materials in the work. He himself would have done so and so. That does not mean that he himself could do it, for he probably lacks the technical skill and training. But he can tell just where he is dissatisfied and why.

Incidentally, this sort of specific judgment also lays the critic himself wide open to criticism. He as well as the artist has shown how he imaginatively handles aesthetic materials. And he may be wrong himself. This mode of criticism accordingly makes the critic very responsible. Actually the critic has to know just as much as the artist about the potentialities of materials, or more. Artist, critic, and spectator all come intimately together in this mode of appreciation and criticism, for they all have the common enterprise of finding the maximum integration and satisfaction for the materials before them.

When a spectator is dissatisfied, then the point of dissatisfaction is open to discussion. In regard to highly integrated works of art nothing is further from the truth than the *de gustibus non est disputandum* adage. When the spectator is dissatisfied, then the question is whether the spectator or the artist was wrong in his imaginative construction. The spectator who follows this method will undoubtedly begin spontaneously to check up his own imaginative reconstruction of the work. He will look for confirmations of his feeling expectations in other parts of his work, or for other expectations which other parts of his work may set up for the detail in question. If he finds the detail integrates with other parts of the work, he will then work back over his own original imaginative construction. Perhaps he slipped somewhere along the way. And then possibly he just does not know some of the potentialities of the materials and in so far is a weak spectator. If that is possible, he will wish to discuss the matter with other spectators so as to benefit from their sources of satisfaction which he is missing.

Now, of course, it was just such a criticism I was carrying on for a certain distance a few minutes ago in connection with Coleridge's lyric. And from the time I spent on the word "bold" you must suspect that something jarred my expectations about it. Something did. And, if you recall what followed, you will see it amounted to tracing out a large number of references from and to that word, and finding that they all confirmed it in its unusual position, and set it in its place in the total structure of the poem. From that vantage point my initial doubt and criticism was dispelled.[7] Coleridge was right and I was wrong. But if the confirmation had failed, the criticism would have stood. Even if I had not been satisfied with my own judgment and had sought the confirmation of other readers, the process would have been the same. And in the end the confirmation of other readers is always sought, for any reader may have inhibitions upon certain sorts of references in a work of art which other readers must fill in.

This recreative conception of criticism has had many exponents since Coleridge first discovered it. Henry James, who besides being one of our best novelists is also one of our best critics, habitually employs it. Percy Lubbock inherited the method from James and explained it in its application to the novel in a little book, *The Craft of Fiction*, that deserves to be even better known than it is. I would like you to hear how Lubbock describes the method:

---

[7] Strangely enough, such confirmed unexpectances are the food of vitality in art. This should be no surprise to us after our transit through contextualistic aesthetics, though the organicist is always a little startled and mystified at them. They are, of course, genuine conflicts of expectation which turn out to be just right in the consummatory achievement. In a surpassingly good lyric like this one there is not a pivotal word that is not a little surprising, and somewhat the more so for turning out to be just right in its relations to all the other words.

The reader of a novel—by which I mean the critical reader—
[he writes], is himself a novelist; he is the maker of a book which
may or may not please his taste when it is finished, but of a book
for which he must take his own share of the responsibility. The
author does his part, but he cannot transfer his book like a bub-
ble into the brain of the critic; he cannot make sure that the critic
will possess his work. The reader must therefore become, for his
part, a novelist, never permitting himself to suppose that the creation of the book is solely the affair of the author. . . . From
point to point we follow the writer, always looking back to the
subject itself in order to understand the logic of the course he
pursues. We find that we are creating a design, large or small,
simple or intricate, as the chapter finished is fitted into its place;
or again there is a flaw and a break in the development, the
author takes a turn that appears to contradict or to disregard
the subject, and the critical question, strictly so called, begins.
Is this proceeding of the author the right one, the best for the
subject? Is it possible to conceive and to name a better? The hours
of the author's labour are lived again by the reader, the pleasure
of creation is renewed.[8]

Before leaving this topic a warning apparently needs to
be given to some who enter upon this mode of criticism. It
is strange that there should be any need of it, for the method
is intrinsically self-regulative. But many excellent recreative
critics have somehow got to setting arbitrary limits to the
range of recreation they allow. Roger Fry is an example. He
seems to me one of the keenest and most rewarding critics
yet to appear in the visual arts. But somehow he got the
notion that the materials of a visual work of art must be
limited to those that stimulate the eye—to colors, lines, planes,
and volumes and, in general, the plastic values. The representative, dramatic, and symbolic values he dubbed "literary"
and by arbitrary definitional fiat excluded them from the
aesthetic field of the visual arts. A generation of lesser critics

[8] Percy Lubbock, *The Craft of Fiction* (New York: Jonathan Cape and
Harrison Smith), pp. 17, 23–24.

has followed him, and those who have stood out against him have generally done so on unconvincing grounds and have not known how to answer him in his own terms.

The answer, of course, in the light of our present analysis, is simple. If the "literary" values integrate in their feeling references with the plastic values, or vice versa, they are intrinsic materials of the work of art. Moreover, an integration of both the representations (let us drop the question-begging "literary") and the plastic values is potentially a larger and richer integration than one that restricts itself to either the one or the other. And lastly, a critic who judges a work of art which in fact is an integration of both types of values, by following out the references of one type only, is bound to be frustrated whenever one of these types leads into the other for its organic fulfillment.

There is a tendency for organic critics to become formalistic like Roger Fry. One feels it a little even in Percy Lubbock. It comes out also in many musical critics, who write sometimes as if they were ashamed of any emotions in music. Of course, this is all absolutely contrary to the spirit of organistic criticism which sets no limits whatever upon the materials integrated so long as they are integrated in the mode of feeling.

Now a few words on the third and last consequence of the organistic criterion of beauty that I earlier alluded to—the interpretation of ugliness. Bosanquet spends his whole last lecture, a third of his exposition, on this question. There is, to be sure, an issue involving the basic categories of organicism in regard to negative values that is troubling Bosanquet. This we need not go into. But out of his struggles with the issue comes a conception of invincible ugliness that will stir up a sympathetic vibration somewhere in the heart of every true artist. Invincible ugliness is aesthetic dishonesty.

First, objects which are not integrations of feeling are, of course, not ugly. They are not negative aesthetic values. They are not aesthetic values at all, since they fall outside the aesthetic field. Secondly, experiences of objects which fail to realize the integrations of feeling potentially contained in them do not impute negative aesthetic values to these objects. Let me refer you back to our analysis of the aesthetic work of art in the previous lecture, and the contrast between the ideal consummatory perception and the partial perceptions on the way to it. So far as one of these partial perceptions is felt as a frustrated integration, it is a negative aesthetic value and ugly to the spectator. But, as Bosanquet says, this only bespeaks a weakness of the spectator. The spectator has not mastered the intricacy of the design, or he cannot yet take the tension of the emotion, or he has not enough width of experience to understand the allusions.

> Intricacy, tension, and width [writes Bosanquet], account for a very large proportion of so-called ugliness, that is to say, of what shocks most people, or else seems to them repellantly uninteresting, or overstrained, or fantastic. All this part of ugliness then seems due to the weakness of the spectator, whether his object is nature or art.[9]

The aesthetic work of art in these instances is not ugly though a spectator's experience of it may be. The beauty of the work of art is a "difficult beauty." And the ugliness of the spectator's response can be overcome by a fuller realization of the work.

Thirdly, what if the aesthetic work of art itself is lacking in complete integration? Bosanquet, like most organicists (and I would guess all but the most recent, and include many contextualists along with them), confuses this situation with the preceding. The confusion comes from a failure to make a complete analysis of the aesthetic work of art such as we

---

[9] *Three Lectures on Aesthetic*, p. 95.

gave in the last lecture. If the artist has not himself succeeded in fully integrating his aesthetic materials and communicating their interrelations through a physical work of art, then the aesthetic work itself is lacking in beauty. The work itself falls short of the total integration of which its materials were capable, and as such it must be regarded as ugly. But still it is not what Bosanquet calls an instance of invincible ugliness. It is an instance of what he might have called a weakness of the artist. Some other artist with these same materials might carry them forward to the consummation of which they were capable.

But, fourthly, we reach invincible ugliness when an artist assembles his materials so as to lead us to expect an imaginative integration and then by some positive action of his own directs us to another end. The end is likely to be something like popular applause, or propaganda, or a chance to make a little more money, or submissiveness to authority, or rebellion and pure cussedness, or even "that last infirmity," fame. For these the artist sacrifices the integrity of his work. So, writes Bosanquet, "the principal region in which to look for insuperable ugliness is . . . the region of insincere and affected art. Here you necessarily have the very root of ugliness." [10] The work itself contains ingredients positively frustrating to beauty. The artist himself probably had the capacity to bring his materials to aesthetic consummation. But he turned aside for an easier reward. The motive can be detected by anyone who can imaginatively follow the materials, and the negative judgment on the work of art is sharpened by a judgment on the character of the artist, the keener in that every artist is open to these temptations, and envies while he repudiates the superficial successes of the artist without integrity.

So out of organicism an aesthetic conscience takes form,

[10] *Three Lectures on Aesthetic*, p. 106.

and we can speak of the dictates of taste. But these are really just the natural movement of the aesthetic imagination undiverted in its aim to achieve an organic integration of feeling —an integration, that is, of the ways in which sensations, images, thoughts, and emotions seek to come together of their own accord about a perceptive center such as a physical work of art.

By way of summary, then, an object of great aesthetic value, on this view, is one that achieves or closely approaches such an integration. Criticism is a following of the path of such achievement and a marking of questionable junctures along the way where frustrations or gaps occur in the experience of the critic. And appreciation is the same thing in the satisfactions of the partial achievements along the way and the triumph of final consummation in the total organic structure. In this imaginative activity artist and critic and spectator are nearly as one. They are a group of travelers all actively following the same trails with one of them, the artist, as their guide. Ugliness, or negative aesthetic value, appears in the accidents or blocks along the way which may be due to the awkwardness of one of the group in not watching the guide, or to a failure of the guide to clear the trail properly, but invincible ugliness occurs when the guide betrays his followers and deliberately leads them astray for some reason of his own.

Whatever may happen to organicism in the future, I think this process of the creative imagination will never be forgotten. It joins artist, critic, and spectator, or all who seek aesthetic values, into a community united in the creation of objects of the highest aesthetic worth.

5

Formistic Criticism

IT SEEMS as though we have run through the whole gamut of criticism in the last three lectures. From the loose, free and easy-going aesthetics of pleasure and sensuous immediacy, through the contextualistic conception of beauty as the realization of a situation in the quality of perception where a work of art is a funded consummation of a succession of perceptions, to the organistic view where beauty is a firmly integrated whole, what other attitudes towards art are possible? Along this line of attitudes, none. But there is something to be considered about the width of the line, so to speak. There is a question of normal pleasures and perceptions as opposed to abnormal. Most people have a conviction that there is something better about a normal perception and judgment of values than an abnormal one, and this is the point that is emphasized in formistic aesthetics and criticism.

It would not be correct to say that this insight has had no recognition in the previous views. In mechanistic criticism, it was pointed out that we can count on a good deal of uniformity in men's judgments about pleasures in things because of the considerable degree of similarity in men's physiological make-up and behavior. In contextualism there was likewise an anticipation of a pretty fair agreement within any cultural epoch about the quality of the final funded perception of a work of art. And in organicism a stable determinate judgment is predicted of any fully integrated work. Any one of these views would admit that a judgment that diverged markedly from the anticipated judgment in the light of human experience might be called abnormal.

The views would differ characteristically in their treatment of such judgments. In mechanism they would be given their full value credit. They would be simply somewhat freakish values, queer things for a person to like. Just possibly there might be a suspicion as to whether the person really liked them and did not have a perverted taste based on hidden fears. But so far as the person feels he enjoys them, they are his values and that is final.

In contextualism, an abnormal judgment would generally be regarded as a failure to take in all the factors of a situation. It would not be condemned for its abnormality but for its inadequacy. In so far as the peculiarities of an individual are concerned, these would be accepted as part of the situation, but the judgment would be supposed to take in the whole situation, those peculiarities included, and the judgment would be abnormal only in a refusal of a person to see himself in the total situation of which he was actually a part.

In organicism, the attitude of contextualism would simply be carried a step further in the insistence that if a person's peculiarities precluded an integration, there must be something abnormal in the situation and a change is demanded either in the person or the other factors of the situation or both to bring about the integration.

There is, then, some evidence for the factual justification of the normal in contrast to the abnormal even in these views which make no effort to justify it. Formism, however, stresses the fact of the normal, seeks to isolate it, and to define value in terms of it. In doing so, it contributes something which the other views tend to submerge.

Formism has had a longer period of dominance in the history of occidental culture than any other relatively adequate philosophy. As the view of Plato and Aristotle (their differences are in the nature of a family quarrel), it was the most persistently influential view in classical thought, and through Augustine and Thomas Aquinas it saturated medieval thought. In spite of the violent reaction against it in the Renaissance, it has maintained a steady though dwindling influence through the modern period. It probably reached its lowest ebb in the nineteenth century, though it was in that very century that it thrust up two of its best representatives in aesthetic criticism—namely Ruskin and Taine. It is significant that neither of these men had an inkling that he was supported by the presuppositions of Aristotle and Aquinas and would have been much troubled had he known it. Ruskin wrapped his formism in a naïve fundamentalism from which he imagined it derived; and Taine concealed his formism behind a bluff exterior of positivistic matter-of-factness. Naturally neither of them could make the most of their theory with such drags, so that the successes of these critics are the more to be noticed as indicative of the latent power of this theory in art, which, to my mind, has never been adequately brought to expression. There is no completely developed formistic book on aesthetics that I know of comparable, for instance, to Santayana's *Sense of Beauty* for hedonism. Aristotle's *Poetics* is the best, and it is excellent, but it is little more than a collection of notes.

Though there is a return of interest in formistic modes of thought, the shadow of Hume falls so heavily over our times that philosophers do not like to declare very loudly that they may be defending a doctrine of the reality of norms. Nevertheless it makes an appearance, even outside of neo-scholastic circles. It is presupposed in such respectable treatments of natural law as W. E. Johnson's in his *Logic*,[1] and is suggested in conceptions of the normal mind such as come out in Price's analysis of perception and S. Alexander's analy-

[1] William Ernest Johnson, *Logic* (Cambridge: The University Press, 1921).

sis of aesthetic judgment. And lately new evidence has appeared for the soundness of the latter conception from quite unexpected quarters. From psychiatry and particularly from psychoanalytical studies we are gradually acquiring a pretty clear picture of the nature and development of a normal personality and of the structure of human values connected with it. These discoveries in conjunction with the evidences of evolution in the formation of species and the traditional evidences have a definite bearing on aesthetic judgment and criticism. And I shall now try to bring these out.

Before coming to close quarters with the question in its bearing on aesthetic value, I should like you to consider the obvious inferences one would make from the table of chemical elements provided a mechanistic or operational philosophy were not dominating the scene. Here we are presented with ninety odd distinct species of matter. There are a few isotopes, but these do not alter the situation. Each element is a cluster of properties, and matter appears on this level of nature in the forms of these distinct species and in no other forms. This is a well attested hypothesis about the physical world, so well attested as generally to be called fact. Nature on this level is not continuous or haphazard or subject to estimates of probability in the distribution of chemical properties. Matter falls definitely into one or another of a limited number of clusters of properties and matter is discontinuous between these property clusters.

Moreover, when we learn of the reason for these discontinuities in theories of the structure of the atom as composed of subatomic elements, the determinateness of the atomic forms is strengthened. They are then seen to be the various structures of equilibrium in which the subatomic elements can be arranged. There are no states of equilibrium intermediate between those states constituting the chemical elements with their resultant properties.

Now, I am going to suggest that a natural norm is such a state of equilibrium together with the properties resulting from it. States of equilibrium are discontinuous in nature, and extend up through all the levels of natural integration. On the higher levels, however, the gaps between the equilibrium states tend to be filled in with structures in more or less unstable equilibrium, so that the picture takes on an appearance of continuity and the state of relatively stable equilibrium becomes a region of slightly varying structures of varying stability rather than a point of one fixed stable structure.

This is the condition of equilibrium states on the level of life. There is a discontinuity of a sort among animal species, but not with such clear gaps as between species of atomic matter. There is a much wider range of variation among the individuals of a species and moreover a certain amount of cross-breeding occurs. However, even apart from the many animal structures like dragons and griffins and centaurs which a fertile imagination can conceive, there are many freaks like double-headed calves and other monstrosities which nature itself conceives, that either cannot exist at all under the conditions of life, or only for a short time.

The significance of such evolutionary factors as the survival of the fittest now begins to be seen. Only those forms of life survive which are in a state of relatively stable equilibrium in respect to their internal organization and the environmental conditions in which they are placed. And under conditions of increased environmental pressure those forms which are in less stable equilibrium will tend to perish and those in more stable equilibrium to survive. The latter are better adapted or more adjustable, which amounts to the same thing. It becomes possible then to describe the characteristics of a form of life in stable adjustment with its habitat, and this is a species. And this description is automatically an empirical norm. Permanent or rigid structural variants from the norm are freaks and the presumption is that the organisms concerned are out of equilibrium and will not survive. If they do survive and propagate, they become recognized as a new species, a new form of stable equilibrium. Temporary variants from the norm are called disease.

Notice that the norm establishes the basis for a judgment of value. A freak is bad and a disease is bad. They are bad because the individual is thrown off a state of vital equilibrium and is likely to perish, or at least more likely to perish than other individuals of his species.

I said a norm of the species becomes a norm of value. There are many who will raise objections to this assertion. I cannot hope to answer all these objections. In so far as they consist in casting doubt on the existence of natural norms, I merely refer back to the evidence for equilibrium states in nature, and the tendency for natural structures such as organisms which lack the characteristics essential for their type of equilibrium to perish.

The real issue is as to whether survival, or, as it affects men, life is a basis for establishing values. The norms of species are those clusters of characters which have such stability that they are able to survive and live in their environment. Structures lacking this stability have perished. The former were adjusted, the latter unadjusted to their environment. Now the issue over the applicability of value to these natural norms —that is to structures capable of survival—comes down to whether value can be defined in terms of adjustment.

Clearly this is different from defining value, for instance, in terms of satisfaction. And the manner of defining value is, we have seen, supremely important, as it constitutes the basic criterion of value once it is determined upon. If value is defined in terms of adjustment, then it follows that satisfactions of interests at variance with the satisfactions characteristic of a normal man are bad, and that so also are objects producing them, many of which would clearly be aesthetic objects. But delaying a little longer our formistic description of aesthetic objects, I here would like you to see clearly what the effect of accepting the norm of the adjusted man is upon, for instance, the popular interest theory of value, and at the same time to note that there is just as good reason in usage and in philosophy for accepting one of these definitions as a basic criterion as the other. That is to say, usage in the form of a common sense test definition justifies quite as much the definition of value in terms of individual adjustment for the sake of the survival of a group or species as it does that in terms of individual satisfactions. And the one has the corroborative support of the formistic world hypothesis quite as much as the other has that of the mechanistic. In short, defining value in terms of a natural norm is as justifiable as defining it in terms of satisfaction of interest.

But what, in particular, would a norm of the human species be? What is a normal man?

It is not an average. If there were a number of diseased people in a group, the average would not be the normal man. For such an average would not be the set of characteristics describing the equilibrium state constituting man as an organism in adjustment with his environment and with capacity of survival as a member of his species.

Secondly, the normal man is not a completely determinate set of characteristics. The norm may allow a man to vary in height by two feet or more, to be blond, brunet, yellow, black, or red, to be pug-nosed, or Roman-nosed, round-headed or long-headed. And the normal female is, of course, different from the normal male. Besides there is no very sharp line between the normal and the abnormal. Many of the attempts to dispose of the conception of a norm of the species consist in requiring absolute determinateness in the characteristics of the norm. This is absurd. In the first place, even if the norm were determinate our empirical knowledge of it would only be to an approximation and to that degree would be indeterminate. But, in the second place, the evidence indicates that the norm admits a range of indeterminacy. Think of it as the condition of vital equilibrium and then a range of indeterminacy is easy to conceive and is to be expected.

In ordinary terms, the normal man is simply the healthy man, healthy in body and mind both. That does not mean that he is necessarily the biggest and strongest. A city boy may be healthier than a farm boy, being more resistant to disease and more adjustable. We are learning more and more about the characteristics of good health year by year. But because we do not know all about it, it would be ridiculous to say we do not know what good health is. The medical men selecting draftees in the present war had a pretty good idea of what they were looking for. They wanted physically and mentally sound men for the fundamental biological reason of their survival value. There was a considerable range of acceptable characteristics, but there were definitely unacceptable characteristics as well as a lot of doubtful cases. And among the unacceptable characteristics were certain likes and dislikes which indicated mental instability. The norm of health took precedence over human interests, and unhealthy interests were judged bad. Don't think I am equating the human norm with the medical requirements for induction into the armed forces. But these requirements are an approximation to it. And note especially that they are not fundamentally man made. They are biologically conditioned. As Darwin has pointed out, nature takes the place of a stock breeder in natural selection. In the end nature always takes the man's place in determining norms of adjustment. This observation is the great contribution of formism, which has a pervasive though often hidden bearing on every aspect of human life including the aesthetic.

Now acknowledging the normal man, let us see how this concept works up into society and social institutions and eventually art.

A complication of the concept arises in that man is normally a social animal, so that a concept of a normal human society gets built on top of that of the normal human organism. The relation between the norm of man and the norm of his society would be simple, if the society were entirely composed of normal men and were the outgrowth of the association of such men under their particular environmental conditions. I venture to say that this does constitute the ideal center of the norm of human society.

But there is evidence that men who would be regarded as far from normal in their individual psychological behavior may through mutual social support more or less successfully maintain a neurosis as a social institution. Of course some would say that a neurosis is not a neurosis if it is socially sanctioned. That is a method of explaining normality away in terms of social conventions, and is rather too easy, and explains too much away. My hypothesis on formistic evidence is that certain types of social equilibrium can be developed out of organisms who as individuals would be considered relatively unstable. Such societies could be regarded as within the range of social normality, though its members as individuals would be abnormal men, or at least abnormal in certain respects.

However, it is fairly clear that human societies which contain large numbers of unstable individuals, even though the grounds of the instability are institutionalized and socially sanctioned, are not likely to be as stable and adjustable as those composed of normal individuals.

The bearing of these remarks on our problem comes out as soon as it is remembered that social structures are reflected and embodied in social institutions and in tools and other

objects created through these institutions. In short, cultures
are the expressions of social structures. In having endured
long enough to have developed institutions and objects which
embody them, a culture proves to have had a stability and
so to fall within the range of social normality. At the same
time some cultures can be considered as superior to others in
terms of their degree of stability. Moreover, it is natural to
believe (though the belief needs confirmation) that the most
stable society would be one composed of the greatest possible number of stable individuals; or, in other words, that
the health of a society is correlated with the health of the
individuals who compose it.

Now let us relate these comments on individual and social
normality to the traditional tenets of formistic aesthetics.
Obviously aesthetic value will have something to do with
conformity to natural norms. There have been three common
ways of defining this conformity.

First, there is the definition of aesthetic value as the representation of a norm. The norm is here generally assumed to
be the norm of the species—the norm for an individual organism. This is the basis of the mimesis theories, defining
beauty as imitation. It applies most clearly to the representative arts, to sculpture, painting, drama, and novel. The imitation, however, is not of a particular individual, but of the
norm which the individual represents. The imitation of the
particular is disparaged by all formists since Plato, including
Plato. The artist sees the universal, the norm, through the
particular, and the beauty of the representation is in proportion to the degree in which the artist has been able to pene-
trate to the universal implicit in the particular and exhibits
the ideal. The artist aims for the essence, the real character
of things, not the depiction of accidental, meaningless details. The work of art itself thus acquires a universality of
value in embodying universal norms, which as permanent po-

tentialities of stability implicit in nature are permanent sources of aesthetic perception.

Second, aesthetic value has been defined as conformity with the norm implicit in the art object itself. This definition applies particularly to the applied arts, and through them to the pure arts (so called), stressing the intrinsic demands of the physical materials of art and craftsmanship. This phase of formism comes very close to organicism. Every object has a potentiality of perfection arising from its suitability to the end it will serve, the capacities of its materials, and the technical skill of the craftsman to shape the materials and make the most of them. The cult of craftsmanship in the middle ages was closely connected with the formistic beliefs of the time. And our loss of interest nowadays in the perfecting of an object may have much to do with our loss of understanding of the insights of formism.

A particular development of this second formistic definition of value is conformity to the *genre*, which generally means a form of composition, but may be extended to include a "style." So critics in the seventeenth and eighteenth centuries spent a lot of time describing literary genres and using them as standards for literary judgment. As norms of literary craftsmanship in specific fields they can be justified, though they are likely to become rigid and can be a source of abuse.

Third, aesthetic value has been defined as conformity to or expression of a culture. This is the side of formism most prevalent today. A work of art has aesthetic value in proportion as it gives expression to its age. This definition tends to run over into a cultural relativism very congenial to contemporary art historians, and in marked contrast to the universality of aesthetic values emphasized in the first formulation of aesthetic value for formism above as representation of the universal.

In the history of formism, critics and writers of aesthetics have emphasized one or another of these formulations of aesthetic value. Can these formulations be brought together? They can, by either of two very simple and ancient definitions. The first defines beauty as the exemplification of a norm. Any natural object, then, is beautiful in proportion as it is a manifestation of its norm. Not only man, but a panther, an oak tree, a minnow, a snail, an earthworm, has a beauty of its own. And extending the principle in consistency with our interpretation of norms as enduring equilibrium states, we see likewise that a molecule, an atom, or an electron has a beauty of its own.

But this definition of beauty is a good deal wider in its field of application than that of the common sense test definition. It makes beauty entirely independent of human existence and human experience. Even though this wider field, on formistic grounds, is shown to include beauty in the commoner, narrower sense, and calls attention to the fact that value in man is an equilibrium state in a generative natural series that has its origin in the structure of an atom, so that in an extended sense of the term an atomic structure could be said to be in the nature of a value, still to equate aesthetic value with so large a field puts an undue strain on the ordinary meaning of the word.

The narrower field is preferable, which finds aesthetic value in human representations and perceptions of norms. As a specific definition of this narrower field (usually pretty vaguely defined) I suggest *perceptions satisfying in themselves to the normal man.* Though one would not at first imagine it, this definition entails all three phases of the traditional formistic aesthetic, and moreover fills up some gaps.

As regards representation, a normal man finds satisfaction in the representation of the traits and the actions of normal men. There is an ancient theory of perception, older even than

Aristotle, which states that only like perceives like. Though this theory does not work in general, it is very nearly true as regards emotional perception. A man appreciates in others what he appreciates in himself. And nowadays with our knowledge of the mechanisms of repression, inhibition, rationalization, transfer, and the like, this truth derives a new emphasis. A repression acts as an emotional blind spot. A man with many repressions not only cannot feel whole areas of other men's values, he cannot even perceive the relations of their acts, and sometimes actually blanks out the acts themselves. Similarly with representations of the types of acts affected. Such a man is, of course, abnormal to the extent that his repressions control his behavior. It follows that only a normal man, with a well integrated and relatively free emotional life, can perceive normality. Moreover, he alone can also perceive abnormality. He perceives it not only because he can contrast it against the background of his own normality, but because in himself he has the impulses which have become exaggerated in the abnormal man and he resonates to the impulses and directly feels their exaggeration.

Now all this applies to art just as much as to everyday experience. A normal man in emotionally perceiving a work of art resonates to what is depicted or expressed there. As soon as he understands the vehicle of expression in the art, he is capable of responding to everything contained in the work, and his responses are balanced and stable. If after a series of funded perceptions he finds satisfaction in the work, that is almost conclusive evidence that the work represents or expresses the human norm. The norm is embodied there, and a normal man finds satisfaction because his impulses are in harmony with the impulses of the work, both being normal. An abnormal man, however, may, on account of his inhibitions or exaggerations of impulse, fail to obtain much satisfaction from the work. That is to say, by defining aesthetic value in terms of the satisfying perceptions of the normal man, it turns out that in fact a work of art is judged according to the degree that it expresses or approximates the norm.

The representation of men as they are seen with the normal eye, penetrating to the traits that count, dwelling seriously on what is serious in life, laughing at what is silly, and altogether showing through the representation a balanced view of human values, that is the representation of the norm. That is what we sense in Shakespeare and Molière, and Rembrandt, and Breughel, and, in another but not ultimately so different a way, in Bach and Beethoven. The representation of the norm is not necessarily in the manner of the direct, naïve conception of the process—namely, a depiction of heroic man. A caricature can strikingly represent the norm if the artist's comment is implicit in the picture and tells just how abnormal the depiction is. And strangely enough a tragedy can represent the norm best of all. It is entirely natural that the tragic flaw theory of tragedy had its origin in Aristotelian thought. For how can you most effectively depict the power of the ideal or normal man? Not by depicting a thoroughly well adjusted man. He makes no mistakes, and the full potentialities of his nature are not made apparent. A weak man, of course, will not do. But depict a strong man who is almost normal but has some flaw. He is over ambitious, he is jealous, he is over reflective and acts too late. In all other respects he has heroic proportions, but this flaw throws him out of adjustment with his environment and precipitates a struggle. Then we see what man can do, and what he is like when he exerts himself to the utmost, and we become aware of man's complete potentialities by perceiving what he would have been without the flaw.

In these ways, our definition of aesthetic value as perceptions immediately satisfying to the normal man literally covers the naïve formistic conception of beauty as the representation of the norm.

It also covers the idea of beauty as the fulfillment of the norm implicit in a fabricated object. For a normal man will find satisfaction in the perception of a well-made object. Normal desires will have normal objects to satisfy these desires, and will require these objects to be well made. Moreover, the normal perception will act as a regulator upon the objects made and the manner of making them. It will have a sense of proportion about things, appreciating function without disparaging decoration, cherishing materials without forgetting their uses. It will not despise machinery nor tradition either. It will recognize many modes of craftsmanship and will not forget that even a craftsman may become a fanatic.

Lastly, our definition covers the formulation in terms of cultural expression and makes a needed correction upon it. A normal man must adjust to his culture, so that inevitably a normal man will find satisfaction in the perception of objects expressive of his times. These are objects of his culture with which he has become identified. But it does not follow that he may not be critical of his culture, aware of traits of instability in it, and dissatisfied with these traits. It is possible for a man to like imperfections as part of something he loves, yet to count them as flaws and really wish they were not there. So, a normal perception critically awake to its times would find a satisfaction of familiarity in all the characteristic traits of the times, even if the age were a relatively unstable one, and yet could also feel dissatisfied with traits which it sensed as unstable. In this way, the aesthetic value in expressing the ideals of an age is accounted for, while at the same time the threat of cultural relativity is avoided, a threat which is inconsistent with the general tenor of formism.[2]

Formism in its stress on the perceptions and reactions of the normal man thus acts as a sort of governor over the whole aesthetic field. It holds art to the healthy golden mean, to what is sane [3] and sound.

Having mentioned the contribution of psychoanalytical studies to this aspect of aesthetic theory, I do not wish to leave the subject without alluding to the catharsis theory, which is one of the most enlightening contributions of formistic philosophy to aesthetics. The essential idea is that emotions get dammed up in the individual through social restraint or personal conscience and need an outlet to restore the organism to equilibrium. Art is one of the most effective means of performing this function. By identifying with the characters of a drama or a novel or with the emotional movement of a piece of music, a man is able to let out his suppressed impulses and gain a vicarious satisfaction. He then feels the pleasure of relief as from a cathartic. The term is Aristotle's, You see how distinctively formistic it is, how it presupposes a normal, healthy state. Art here more than expresses or represents the norm. It has insight into man's emotional requirements and actively returns him to the norm.

[2] Taine in his *History of English Literature* is involved in this problem, especially if his *History* is read against the background of "The Ideal in Art." He makes use of "the representative man" as something between the norm of the species and a fair sample of the man's age. In my interpretation the normal man is definitely the norm of his species, and it is assumed that a fully normal culture would arise from a society of normal men. Hence the judgment of the normal man legitimately legislates over any cultural trait.

[3] But do not think this affords a justification for the present Sanity in Art movement. There is just enough justification for the movement to make it a little dangerous. Judging the movement by its works—that is, its exhibitions—I should say its members were fully as neurotic and abnormal as the most abnormal of those it protests against. A fanatical reactionary is just as abnormal as a fanatical radical. A cult of timidity and dullness is as troublesome to social health as one of fury and shock.

The catharsis theory has many implications for criticism. The tragic and the comic now appear in a new light. It is now part of a critic's function to see how effectively they perform their regulative task and to look into the nature and the source of the conflicts they relieve. The danger from the aesthetic angle here is that criticism may turn into diagnosis. This, however, should be only the beginning of the critical task, for the critic's aesthetic aim is not merely to analyze an artist's complexes, nor to bring out the social problems which contribute to them, nor (what also would be of great value but has scarcely been broached since Plato in his *Republic* and Aristotle in his *Politics* noted its importance) to examine the emotional needs of the public for the health of society—the critic's aesthetic aim is to bring these all together in a judgment of the effectiveness and worth of the work of art in establishing emotional balance and in attaining for the individual the satisfactions of normality.

As an illustration of how this criticism works, consider the exploitations of the repressed materials of dreams and fantasies popular in the pictures of many expressionists today. These pictures have practically no cathartic effect. It has been noted that critics with a psychoanalytic bent have shown very little interest in such pictures. There is good reason for it. The critics prefer to study Leonardo, Michelangelo, El Greco, Böcklin, Rousseau, Picasso. These men have been skillful technicians of catharsis. They know how to draw out a man's repressions without frightening him too much, and so to lead him to experience something sublime rather than repulsive. Dali, for instance, is merely a realist of particulars like Zola but in another field of subject matter. He is a supreme technician in nearly everything but catharsis. He paints the particular details of his particular dreams just as Meissonier painted the particular buttons of particular cavalrymen. Dali and Meissonier are very much alike. They are good imitators of the particular but they have very little sense of the universal.

Inevitably a critic who is searching for the universal in art and for the norm will be only superficially interested in the particulars. He is not much concerned with what one man one time saw or dreamt. But he values anything that leads to human balance and adjustment and the satisfactions of normal functioning. It follows that in the end for him art criticism comes very close to ethical judgment. Plato's insistent bracketing of the Good and the Beautiful as supreme human values turns out to have been a penetrating insight. For art can be a tremendous moral influence.

On our interpretation of the formistic view, then, art represents and gives expression to the natural norm by giving satisfaction to the normal man. This normal man is not an average, but the biological and psychological—that is, the descriptively arrived at—ideal man. The closer a work of art comes to the representation, expression, and consequently to the satisfaction of this normal man, the better it is.

6

How the Four Types of Criteria Operate Together

IN THE PREVIOUS LECTURES we have examined the empirical basis of criticism in the four most adequate world hypotheses at our disposal. We have discovered four different definitional criteria and their relevant standards. In this final lecture I should like to show how these instruments work in practice.

Let me say at once that I do not set myself up as an expert critic in any field of art. All that I shall do is to employ the criteria we have discovered upon such perceptions as I have attained of certain works of art. It is, of course, part of the thesis of this study of criticism that the judgment of a work of art is a cumulative affair, so that no matter how great a man's experience it needs to be supplemented and checked by the perceptions of other men. My perceptions, therefore, will simply require a little more supplementation than those of more experienced men. The method may be even better exemplified through perceptions such as mine than if they were more expert, for it will show how the method itself, through the variety and mutually compensating character of its critical instruments, sharpens one's perception and induces balance of judgment.

I have selected for our purpose a couple of sonnets. One of the sonnets is taken from among Shakespeare's best, if we may trust the testimony of long literary judgment; the other is one of Hopkins', where the literary judgment is more uncertain.

The comparison will, I think, be illuminating of a number of things.

The way of applying our method will be very literal and pedestrian. I shall ask myself for each work of art what in turn would be the pure mechanistic, the pure contextualistic, the pure organistic, and the pure formistic judgment. Then from the array of these pure judgments, I shall ask what is, so to speak, the total or synthetic judgment of the value of the work. This postrational eclectic judgment is perhaps the one that most interests us at this point. Let us see how it is reached and what it looks like in the two instances before us.

Here is Shakespeare's sonnet:

> When to the sessions of sweet silent thought
> I summon up remembrance of things past,
> I sigh the lack of many a thing I sought,
> And with old woes new wail my dear time's waste.
> Then can I drown an eye, unus'd to flow,
> For precious friends hid in death's dateless night,
> And weep afresh love's long since cancell'd woe,
> And moan th' expense of many a vanish'd sight.
> Then can I grieve at grievances forgone,
> And heavily from woe to woe tell o'er
> The sad account of fore-bemoanèd moan,
> Which I new pay as if not paid before.
> >   But if the while I think on thee, dear friend,
> >   All losses are restor'd and sorrows end.

(1) *Judgment of the Mechanist:* What immediate pleasures are to be found in this poem? Let us begin by running over the principal kinds of pleasures generally to be found in works of art.

There are first the pleasures of the senses such as the pleasures in sounds and in the pulse of rhythm. Among these may perhaps also be counted the pleasures of emotions regarded as vaguely discriminated combinations of internal sensations.

Secondly, there are the pleasures of association, such as arise from words as symbols. Some of these associations produce images, visual, auditory, tactile, and so on; but some produce imageless thoughts which, if they thicken out beyond the bloodless symbols of a page, are probably tentative anticipations and apprehensions.

Thirdly, there are the pleasures of design. Negatively, principles of design are means of avoiding the boredom of monotony—the principles of contrast, gradation, theme-and-variation. But positively they can intensify sense qualities and increase the pleasures that can be found in them.

Fourthly, there are the pleasures of pattern. These are the pleasures arising from attention, the pleasures that come from ease of comprehension when the elements of a work fit comfortably within the structure and limits of attention. For the human attention is limited to the apprehension of from five to eight simple elements, and asks for human comprehensibility that complex objects be organized in groups of groups of groups of not over five to eight elements in a group.

The combination of design and pattern is often called form or the principle of variety in unity. Design gives the variety and pattern the unity, and the two must coöperate to avoid on the one hand monotony, and on the other confusion.

Fifthly, there are the pleasures of recognition or of the fulfillment of type. Our mind is full of concepts, groups of associated meanings and sensuous qualities such as our concepts of pine trees, meadows, clouds, features of men and women, and human character. The fulfillment of these furnishes the pleasures of representative art. There are also types of the uses of things applying to tools, bridges, ships, dwellings. The fulfillment of these gives us pleasures in satisfaction of function. And there are types of form, like the sonata form in music, and the sonnet form in poetry. And many other sorts of types.

Sensations, images, design, pattern, and type—these are the principal sources of aesthetic delight. All these pleasures are to be found exemplified in Shakespeare's sonnet. The beauty of the sonnet comes from the continuous flow of such pleasures. We read it over and over and new pleasures constantly open up to us and afterwards in memory they return to delight us. It is not that we may count the sources of stimulation. That is not feasible. But the multitude and concentration of the stimuli and their mutual cumulative effect can be clearly felt, and in samples can be demonstrated. Moreover, many of these pleasures are intense and the total effect is one of great pleasure. Of course, I am assuming a receptive reader approaching the poem for its aesthetic stimulation. Let us examine some samples.

Consider its sensuous character. It flows with ease in the reading. Over an underlying five stress pulsing of iambic meter broad explicit rhythms of speech follow the movement of thought and emotion. There is constant rhythmic variety from line to line. In the first line, after a light initial shock from an unexpected accent on "when," heavy beats gather towards the end of the line

"When to the sessions of sweet silent thought."

Then the rhythm spreads rather evenly over the whole second line

"I summon up remembrance of things past,"

a tension gathered up at the end of the first line is relieved in the second. Then the third line is almost perfectly regular, releasing the tension still further. But the fourth line (following its thought) fairly drags with heavy accents against the underlying meter.

"And with old woes new wail my dear time's waste."

And so the rhythm alternates between tension and relaxation, giving pleasure of contrast with each timely shift. And simultaneously there is the pleasure of the congruence of thought and emotion with the rhythmic changes, a pleasure of slightly surprised recognition.

Turn to the sounds themselves, the pleasant sequences of the consonants and vowels. I pass over the rhymes which are obvious. The poem is rich in alliteration and assonances, the *s*'s in the first three lines, the *w*'s in the fourth, and so on. Moreover, note the appropriateness of these alliterated noises to the thoughts expressed. Similarly note the soft *e*'s and *a*'s in the first two lines and the open *o*'s and *a*'s in the fourth in their relation to the thoughts expressed. The sequence of vowels and consonants will also bear observation for their easy transitions, and gradations, and contrasts. Take $\bar{ee}$, $\bar{\imath}$, $\breve{e}$, $\breve{o}$ at the end of the first line, $\breve{a}$, $\breve{\imath}$, $\bar{\imath}$, $\breve{o}$ at the end of the third, $\bar{\imath}$, $\bar{ee}$, $\bar{\imath}$, $\bar{a}$ at the end of the fourth, $\bar{\imath}$, $\breve{u}$, $\bar{oo}$, $\bar{o}$ at the end of the fifth. They are all easy transitions, but also they echo one another.

And now consider the imagery and thought which are the special medium of poetry. One of the charms of such a poem is the profusion of its images like a field full of flowers. Associations spring up on all sides from the symbols and the sounds, and at the same time the thought moves steadily through the images leading to a unity without confusion. Pick a few of the most striking images: "Sessions of sweet silent thought," "my dear time's waste," "death's dateless night." These are the more remarkable in that the ideas they image are very abstract. "Sessions of sweet silent thought" are periods of revery. Shakespeare substitutes for the abstract symbol, symbols of pleasant associations that spring out of it. From these latter symbols we associate backward to the abstract idea but also forward to the pleasant things Shakespeare wants us to think of: to "sweetness" with its associations of honey and kindly affection; to "silence" with its associations of peace and calm; to "sessions" with its associations of companionship and intimate communication; to "thought" with its associations of inwardness and freedom from the outside world. These, at least, are my present associations that fill out the image of this phrase and make it a sweet thing to hold in the mind.

Note, too, how this sort of poetic guidance of our associations transmutes the thought of a depression which is the main subject matter of the poem into something glorious and entrancing. "Death's dateless night" shows the way of this transformation most clearly. The idea is grief for his lost friends. But the great emptiness of death becomes under the poet's guidance the glory of a moonless and perhaps cloudless night under the changeless stars, the static symbol of eternity. The condensed beauty of the phrase, its sounds as well as its sense add to the effect — for observe the two *d*'s and the two *t*'s and the assonance on the muted *e*, the same *e* that was an assonance in the first lines. And mouth the phrase and see how smoothly each sound moves into its successor, the *s* carries the tongue from *th* back toward the *d*, and the long *a* prepares it to take the *t* whence it slips into the *l*, the *e* follows easily and from *s* the tongue slides back into the nasal *n*, opens for the English diphthong *i* (*ä—ee*) and then closes naturally on *t*. It is a pleasure just to go through the muscular movements of the phrase. And all this had its associative effect on the image, to reduce the harshness of death.

As for the design of the poem, it is based on a contrast of thought and emotion between the sadness of the first three quatrains and the joy at the recollection of the friend in the final couplet. There is a sense of emotional gradation rising through the quatrains, and the couplet is expected as a climax and comes with the extra surprise of a contrasting joy. The joy is the greater for the preceding sadness. Suspicion of monotony nowhere approaches.

Likewise there is no question of the poem's unity. Its pattern of three quatrains with alternate rhymes and a final couplet, all in iambic pentameter, is well within the easy grasp of attention.

As for types and the pleasures of recognition, the poem is full of them. There is the recognition of technical mastery of the English language and the versification and the poetic handling of words. There is also the recognition of the fulfillment of the sonnet form as a stereotyped pattern. Given the pattern, the thought fits it with a neatness that is a delight in itself. But the type I wish particularly to call attention to is that of representation. The poem is, as we say, true to life. It represents a mood that everyone has gone through. As much as if it were a painted portrait, we say to ourselves, "How like one of us it is." Moreover, it is a rather detailed description of the mood and indicates that Shakespeare has searched into himself and man's nature. It is not a superficial likeness but a penetrating one. In proportion to its depth, it delights us.

Such are among the pleasures to be found in this poem. Are there also displeasures? The thought is, to be sure, sad and so far unpleasant. But we recognize its inevitability in the nature of human life, and the pleasure in recognizing how truly it is depicted goes far to compensate for its unpleasantness. Moreover, the theme is softened by the charms of sound, rhythm, and imagery, and is rounded in the end by a pleasant thought which makes up for a lot of the sadness. It should not be forgotten also that there is a degree of pleasure for many people in sadness itself if the mood is not too intense. There seem to be no other unpleasantnesses.

Altogether the poem exhibits an exceptional capacity for pleasant stimulation and this increases with added discrimination. It is an exceptionally fine poem.

(2) *Judgment of the Contextualist:* The details pointed out

in the preceding account by the mechanist are all aesthetically significant. But the mechanist puts the wrong emphasis upon them and misses their genuine aesthetic significance. It is their vividness of quality that makes them important in the poem. Their pleasantness is merely the limitation within which quality may be easily appreciated.

What needs to be noted in all these details is their freedom from banality, their freshness which in general arises from stresses and conflicts in their contexts. The conflicts have to be so adjusted that, while they break through the dullness of habit and custom, they do not break out into practical action. This generally means that they must not be very painful. But a little pain is often a spur to vivid perception.

The sadness of the theme is a case in point. This is an emotional fusion of suggested frustrations. The poet calls the conflicts out, "old woes," "dear time's waste," "precious friends" gone. The very intonation and rhythms of the phrases, the muffled vowels ("summon up remembrance"), and the wailing vowels and consonants further support the emotion. But the writer keeps it well below the threshold where it would become too painful and prompt a decisive practical action such as closing the book. In fact, he takes no chances and ends on a bright note, which by its contrast (a mode of conflict) makes its own contribution to vivid perception. We are prompted to read the poem immediately again. The theme of sadness is no demerit but a positive aesthetic quality in the masterful vividness with which Shakespeare draws it out through its weary length and even accentuates it with the brightness of the final couplet, all without aesthetic weariness. The quality of world weariness is vividly produced without weariness in the reader.

While we are on this point, observe that we have stumbled on the total fused quality, the unique quality, of the poem— name it how you will—world weariness, dejection, worry,

but warmed with love in the specific manner Shakespeare
makes you feel. And note how all the details merge and converge into this specific quality. Nothing disturbs it or breaks
into it. It is a splendid harmony of cumulative conflicts.

In saying this our judgment is really made, though one
could go on indefinitely pointing out the hidden or half-
hidden conflicts that make each detail vivid, and the structures
of design and pattern and type that spread the quality and
give it breadth. We might note the adjustment of conflicts
that makes the words, "sessions," "sweet," "silent," and
"thought" so vivid in each other's company, and makes the
quality of the total phrase so haunting. We might go through
the sonnet line by line and word by word. We might try to
list all the inner contrasts of thought ("*old* woes *new* wail
my *dear* time's *waste*") and of sound, and rhythm. We should
learn much about the techniques of a poet in making ideas
and images alive. But time is lacking and we must leave most
of this to the reader's intuition.

I will analyze just one line:

"For precious friends hid in death's dateless night."

I select this line because the mechanist was so afraid of making
it unpleasant that he only partially realized its beauty. He was
so anxious to cover over with charm the bitterness of the
thought of death that he would not let the full quality of the
bitterness come out. His associations went to a cloudless night
among the stars and steadfastness of eternity. Is it not rather a
starless night? Is not a star like a date fixed in the long arc of
time? But this night is dateless, starless, murky, utterly without anything upon which eye or thought could rest. In this
night precious friends are hid beyond hope of recovery. Why
not let the full quality of irretrievable loss rise in our intuition?
Does not the line gain in power and depth? Then the contrast
(conflict) of precious friends and empty night takes com-

plete effect. A starlit night is still precious. But this night of death is empty.

Note too how "hid" goes with "precious," and there seems to be a thought that the friends might have been hidden away against the robbery of death, and then the bitterness that instead it is death that has taken them and hidden them. And how excellently balanced the stress of the word "hid." Substitute "lost," which would be the usual word in that context. How flat it becomes!

Altogether as contextualists, we judge the poem exceptionally rich and vivid in quality.

(3) *Judgment of the Organicist:* Now I come to the poem as an organicist. It does not, of course, from this view make much difference where we start upon the poem. But let us begin with the theme. The contextualist stated it well if somewhat emotionally. It is the feeling of a man in depression over adversity suddenly lifted at the thought of a dear friend. The pattern of the Shakespearean sonnet is obviously perfectly adapted to such a theme. The form might almost have suggested the theme.

The fitness of the imagery and the selections of sounds and rhythms have already been remarked on by the previous judgment. But the remarks were rather general and spotty. They missed the high degree of integration of all the imagery within itself and of all sound within itself and of each with each other that the poem contains. Such internal connections among the features of the poem binding its multitude of details together into a single organic structure are what make it the unique, individual, and nearly perfect work of art that it is.

I am picking out two remarkable instances of such organic structure in this poem. My first instance applies to its imagery. Neither of the previous judgments noticed the inner ties among all the main images of the poem, all due to their connection with money and debts. We sensed an inner appropriateness of the images to one another. They felt integrated. But the internal connections were not clear. Sometimes in poems they are very recondite and hard to expose for analysis even though our feelings respond to them. But in this poem we can trace them openly. They are all details in the metaphor of a merchant's debts. Now we have the key to the connections in terms of the merchant metaphor, consider "sessions," "summon," "old," "new," "dear," "waste," "unused," "precious," "date," "long since cancelled," "expense," "grievances," "heavily," "tell o'er," "account," "pay," "lossses are restored." These images springing from the metaphor are then all one connected image, and from it like leaves from branches of a tree depend all the other images of the poem. Moreover, notice how apt, how connected, this legal and commercial image is with the theme of the poem. From the misery of threatened bankruptcy all losses may be restored to the poor man if some one remaining piece of property proves sound in value.

There is a similar interconnectedness traceable among the principal vowel sequences of the poem. Recent physical experiments have shown that there is a scale of vowels running roughly $\bar{oo}\ \bar{o}\ \d{a}\ \ddot{a}\ \breve{a}\ \bar{a}\ \bar{ee}$. The vowels on the left are low in pitch (that is, the main energy of their sound is concentrated on a region of low pitches) while those on the right are high in pitch. In other words, $\bar{oo}$ and $\bar{o}$ are low pitched vowels on a musical instrument, while $\bar{ee}$ is high pitched like the high tones of a musical instrument. It is furthermore recognized that low tones are intrinsically heavy, fearsome, and even lugubrious, while the high tones are emotionally light, gay, and frolicsome.

With these connections in mind, mark the sequences of the predominant vowels through the course of the sonnet. It starts gently on muted high vowels. In the fourth line two $\bar{o}$'s come ominously in, "old woes," the heavier for their opposition in both thought and sound to "dear time's waste." The next line has "drown" and "flow." Then a muted line. Then "woe" with a contrasted "weep." And in the next immediately "moan." Then "grieve" twice against "foregone." And then three $\bar{o}$'s in a line "woe to woe tell o'er." And then once again three $\bar{o}$'s "fore-bemoaned moan." And another $\bar{o}$, "before," in the last line of this last quatrain, which contains the climax of the poet's grief. There is a steady gradation toward the low vowels corresponding with the emotional gradation towards lower and lower depression. One can see it just in the rhymes—all four rhyming words are on $\bar{o}$ in the last quatrain, two on $\bar{o}$ in the second, none in the first. Such a monotony of rhyming on a single vowel would be a blemish in any other poem. But here it is so integrated with thought and emotion that what would be a fault is transformed into a virtue. The poet is obsessed with this lugubrious tone just as he is with his lugubrious thought. Then suddenly he thinks of his friend. With this thought the long $\bar{o}$ disappears and the bright $\bar{ee}$ is repeated twice just before "friend," "thee, dear friend." In the last line the $\bar{o}$ comes back again with the thought of losses though "restor'd," but it has not the emphasis that rolled up on it in the final quatrain.

Did Shakespeare know he was doing this? That is an irrelevant question. In a way, yes, inevitably. In another way, no. The grounds of these connections have only recently come out in the study of timbre, some centuries after Shakespeare wrote his sonnet and embodied them. But the poet in him definitely was working in the materials of the poem and through their intrinsic connections towards their perfect integration. Emotion and theme and words and images and sounds all drew towards one another for mutual satisfaction in an individual organic structure.

While on this subject, let me note another connection that gently binds the ending of the sonnet with its beginning. The final rhyme of the couplet "friend-end" is on the same muted *e* that was the first vowel assonance in the poem "When . . . sessions . . . silent . . . remembrance." Incidentally, it is also the assonance in that most poignant line, "For precious friends hid in death's dateless night."

That this poem is highly integrated and rich in the materials integrated there can be no question. Is there any break anywhere in the structure?

I do feel a little gap of inappropriateness somewhere. Is it that there is something a trifle flippant about the couplet? Or is it the quatrains that lay it on a little too thick? Or is the whole poem not quite serious enough, as if Shakespeare were displaying his magnificent talent over an occasion rather than speaking out of it. This is the peril of virtuosity, and Shakespeare sometimes succumbs to it, and possibly there is just a tinge of purple here. If so, a slight flaw of character integration works into the poem and detracts in some degree from its complete potential organicity.

But admitting some little weakness of this sort, we cannot deny that the poem approaches very nearly to its full capacity of aesthetic integration, or, in other words, its own unique form of perfection.

(4) *Judgment of the Formist:* As a formist I now ask about the normality of the poem. How well does it represent its culture? Is it a well-made object fulfilling its function or its *genre?* How satisfying is it to a fully developed highly discriminating man? Of these the last, we saw, is the crucial one. The first question need not detain us, for this poem raises no serious problem of cultural discrepancies. It is admired today probably very much as it was admired in its own time. As to the second question, the earlier judgments abundantly show that it fulfills its genre of the Shakespearean sonnet and is an excellent piece of literary craftsmanship.

We need to consider carefully only the last and crucial

question. And here no problem appears to present itself. The poem is an expression of a normal emotional reaction to a frustrating situation. It depicts the instinctive attitude of grief in the recollection of irretrievable loss, and the sudden comfort that comes in the thought of love. The poem taps basic instincts and truthfully describes them as the normal man would exhibit them. We all recognize ourselves in this sort of situation, and are elevated, so to speak, in sharing in this expression of our own basic nature and capacities, and, if we are under similar stress, we may experience catharsis. It is a supremely good poem, in that sense of goodness characteristic of formism in which the aesthetic and the moral come very close together. For it is a poem that induces balance and adjustment of character in the reader.

In the judgment of the formist, on all scores this is a very great poem.

For the purpose of comparison, let us now consider a sonnet by Hopkins in the light of these four philosophical views.

> I wake and feel the fell of dark, not day.
> What hours, O what black hoürs we have spent
> This night! what sights you, heart, saw; ways you went!
> And more must, in yet longer light's delay.
>   With witness I speak this. But where I say
> Hours I mean years, mean life. And my lament
> Is cries countless, cries like dead letters sent
> To dearest him that lives alas! away.
>
>   I am gall, I am heartburn. God's most deep decree
> Bitter would have me taste: my taste was me;
> Bones built in me, flesh filled, blood brimmed the curse.
>   Selfyeast of a spirit a dull dough sours. I see
> The lost are like this, and their scourge to be
> As I am mine, their sweating selves; but worse.[1]

[1] *Poems of Gerard Manley Hopkins*, edited with notes by Robert Bridges, Second Edition (Oxford University Press, 1931).

(1) *Judgment of the Mechanist:* On first reading this affects me as a disagreeable poem. It is obscure in meaning, rough in rhythm, and bitter and disgusting in such images as break through the crust of its perverse diction. This being the initial response, suppose we go on looking for disagreeable things and see if along the way there are enough delights to compensate the irritation. If a poem were to be judged by one reading, I should say on hedonic grounds this is an ugly poem, and I would never return to it.

But as a critic I want to know just how ugly it is, and moreover my experience tells me I may be deceived in a first reading and from lack of discrimination miss pleasures that lie beneath a repellent exterior. So let us examine the poem feature by feature as we did Shakespeare's sonnet.

What of its sensuous character? On closer examination we find a surprising quantity of pleasurable sound. It is unusually rich in the sensuous trappings of sound, in assonance, alliteration, rhyme, and other unnamed subleties. Of the last, consider within line two "hours" (one syllable) with "hoürs" (two syllables) acting as an inner rhyme of a kind, and within line three "night" and "sights," and within line six "hours-years," and perhaps in lines seven and eight "countless . . . dearest." Note too how the assonance falls in line eleven on the three accented participles only

"Bones bu̲ilt in me, flesh f̲illed, blood br̲immed the curse,"

and how the parallel nouns modified by these participles alliterate with them, and how the parallelism is rhythmically stressed by the spondees. I pass over all the more obvious assonances and alliterations that weave through the poem.

Moreover, taking the poem phrase by phrase, the sound sequences are often amazingly sonorous and fitted for smooth articulation. We discover a master technician at work. The first line is a marvelous flow of sounds, and the fourth, and the fifth, and the eighth, and the ninth. The poet obviously has an unusual sensitivity for the musical powers of verse. How, then, can he produce a phrase like:

"Selfyeast of a spirit a dull dough sours"

or

"Cries countless, cries like dead letters sent"

which are both cacophonous and tongue-knotting?

In rhythm the same sort of perverseness is apparent, but worse. The only rhythmically smooth lines are the first and the thirteenth and even these are marred by a monotony of monosyllables. The whole poem is, in fact, monosyllabic. This has much to do with its rhythmical jerkiness. But of all the lines, hear this one:

"This night! what sights you, heart, saw; ways you went!"

It is the jerks he gives in his rhythms that obscure the sonority of his sounds, and, in fact, everything else that might be noticed, just as it is hard to enjoy a mountain view if one is being bumped all the time over a corduroy road. Though this poem contains many potential pleasures, they are scarcely noticeable among the irritations.

Turning to the associative features—the thought and the images—we discover a similar situation. The thought is awfully hard to get at. If one adjusts oneself to the semipractical attitude of treating the subject matter of this poem as a puzzle, one can get a semiaesthetic pleasure in the exercise of solving the puzzle. But when the puzzle is solved one is a little disappointed at the simplicity of the thought. It appears that Hopkins had experienced a bad night, a case of insomnia, and was suffering from an imaginary sense of being abandoned. It is like writing a poem on the miseries of a boil or a stomach ulcer. It is not a pleasant subject anyway. But why add the annoyance of being obscure about it? Everybody knows what insomnia is and many people have experienced it. Why not out with the subject plainly and then make it as pleasant as it can be made? That is what Shakespeare did with his troubles in his sonnet.

And the images. What images!—"fell of dark," "black hours," "cries countless," "dead letters," "gall," "heartburn," "bitter taste," "bones . . . flesh . . . blood," "curse," "sour dough," "scourge," and "sweat." Grant an imagination of much poetic capacity, why use it this way without any compensation of charm or dignity? Compare these unalleviated leaden metaphors with "death's dateless night" which envelops an idea much sadder than insomnia but has a lift in it.

We will leave the poem's pattern and design as neither good enough nor bad enough for comment.

We come to the values of recognition. There are possibilities of pleasure here in the fulfillment of the Petrarchan sonnet form, in the veridical representation of an experience, and in the recognition of technical excellencies.

As to the first, the best we can say is that the form is passably fulfilled but without distinction. A break in the thought does come suitably for the break in the form; the octet describes a situation and the sestet the reaction to the situation. The rhymes, however, are commonplace (rhymes on $\bar{a}$ and $\overline{ee}$ consume over half the rhyming words), where we except a choiceness in so choice a poetic form. And a question may be raised as to the appropriateness of the couplets tinkling inside the sestet. They weaken the contrast with the octet and unbalance the structure of the poem. There is no apparent justification for their presence. Moreover the violent irregularities of rhythm are entirely inappropriate to the form. Altogether there is no pleasure to be got from it.

As to truth to human experience, here lies the main chance for the poem. Does Hopkins so faithfully describe the sufferings of insomnia in an overwrought man that we can delight in the recognition of the fact, however disagreeable the fact itself may be? I think we must admit that he does. If we have perseverance to endure the content of the poem and to work out and take in its meaning, there is no question that in a highly condensed form Hopkins has given a vivid picture of his horrible night.

As to the pleasures in the recognition of technical skill, the poem is potentially full of them. Hopkins is clearly a master craftsman. But he employs his craft so unevenly, not to say obstreperously, that one becomes as much annoyed at his skill as delighted. A poet whose imaginative gifts can so convincingly give eyes to a heart, link "dead letters" with prayers to God, identify orthodox hell with a man's self-inflicted fright, could well use this talent to more delightful advantage. And a man whose command of words and sounds can fill the interior of his poem with such excessive ornament of euphony could well bestow equal attention to the pattern and harmony of his outer rhymes.

All in all, it is a bad poem. The first impression is bad. I mean it is repelling and unpleasant. With more discrimination, one discovers many amazingly pleasing features, evidences of exceptional poetic skill, vigorous imagination, and a power of realism. But the poem is unnecessarily obscure in expression, disagreeable in subject matter, unrelieved and heavy in treatment, jerky in rhythm, and slovenly in what you might call ordinary good manners in versification.

(2) *Judgment of the Contextualist:* The discriminations of the mechanist may be taken over bodily. But his judgment of their aesthetic value is utterly distorted by his prejudice for charm. And his prejudice blinds him to a whole set of obvious details, which he passed over.

The poem is one of exceptional beauty. It is a condensed vivid perception, with a rich highly fused quality of great depth. The more one enters into the texture of the work, the more it gains in richness.

The distastefulness of the experience is irrelevant, so long as it has vividness and depth and can be dwelt upon. The poem is undoubtedly severe and makes demands on even an experienced reader. The poem is not one that would be popular. But neither is it unendurable. It is simply too effective and probing to be endured by *some* people, whose range of appreciation or aesthetic tolerance has not yet expanded enough to intuit it.

Its initial obscurity is also irrelevant. It is effective at the first reading and grows increasingly so, as its meanings reach out further and further. The mechanist wholly misses the significance of the strands that reach out into the great Christian tradition of Church and God and heaven and hell and the place of man in that world. The experience of a soul that fears it is deserted in the context of that tradition is the inner subject of Hopkins' poem and the depth of that fear is as great as the extent of the tradition it exemplifies. All the depth and extent of that tradition enter into the quality of Hopkins' experience.

Moreover, he has realized this quality fully, even beyond what one would conceive possible from the subject, and he has communicated the quality with great technical skill. He is a master of the technique of creating vividness by conflicts of meaning and at the same time holding the texture of his poem together by those very conflicting strands of meaning. The poem is a fine illustration of the harmony of conflicts. Take the first line for an example of this principle in a detail,

> "I wake and feel the fell of dark, not day."

Note the opposition of "wake" and "day" to "feel the fell of dark." "Wake" and "day" are visual, expansive, light; what is opposed is tactile, confined, heavy, and sightless. What he wants is a fresh awakening on a bright morning after a peaceful sleep; what he gets is wakefulness at night and a beastly ("fell") feeling of dread and depression. The opposed meanings are interwoven into one thought, and mutually enhance every thread of the thought. And note the effect of enclosing the dark thought within the light one, placing "the fell of dark" between "wake" and "day."

I pass over the startling "black hoürs" in the second line except to remark on the double stress on "hoürs" forced against the conventional pronunciation, and against the ordinary "hours" uttered at the beginning of the line, even against the rhythm of the line by the very paradox of a monosyllable being violently pulled into a dissyllable so as to conform to the line. See what all this does to the realization of the interminableness of those "hoürs." [2]

But I do wish to call your attention to the "we" in "we have spent" in contrast to the "I" which opened the poem. The "we" means Hopkins and his heart split apart and in conflict and yet also indissolubly united in the meaning of that very word "we."

This sort of thing is going on all through the poem. It attains a climax in the last thought of the poem—that hell itself is just this inner conflict and self punishment of a soul in contrast to the traditional conception of an overt hell with disembodied bodies scourged by devils. But this vivid sophisticated idea, which would be almost a solution of the conflict for an emancipated man, is suddenly opposed again and thrown back into a real old fashioned hell again with the unexpected final words "but worse."

A new depth of quality opens up in the pathos of the poem, the inability of so much of modern man to free himself from a myth which he knows is a myth and yet cannot help believing is still real. The man is in conflict with his religion in the very expression of his implicit faith in it. The poem expresses not only the projection of an ancient tradition into our

[2] Does not the word also suggest a canine howl?

modern day but the conflict of that tradition with our time.

As to the roughness of the verse and that mad metaphor of the yeast and the other metaphors the hedonist objects to, these should be considered in their contexts, and I believe they can all be justified in their places for the vividness they yield. But time will not permit us to examine them in detail. Naturally, they are not pretty, but neither is the experience that is being realized through them.

The poem is a great poem, and comparable to the best of Shakespeare.

(3) *Judgment of the Organicist:* The poem is rich in material and rather highly integrated, but by no means comparable to Shakespeare's sonnet. As the contextualist has pointed out, the metaphors and the rhythms and the sounds consistently carry the thought along. This has not always been fully brought out by the previous critics. For instance, notice the connection of the word "fell" having the literal meaning of "skin of a beast," with the sound of the past of "fall." The meaning of "fall" underlies and reinforces "fell" and reaches to the key of the poem's thought. It reappears at the very end in the idea of "the lost," those who have fallen from God's grace.

Moreover, there hovers over his poem the metaphor of a judgment: "with witness" in the fifth line, and "God's most deep decree," and finally the "scourge" and reference to "the lost." This metaphor is integral to the main thought and might well have been drawn through all the figures of the poem, as Shakespeare carried through his merchant's metaphor.

Other integrative features have been commented on previously and are clear enough—the linkage of sound, the consistently broken rhythms and distraught utterance characteristic of a disturbed mind, the organizing power of the sonnet form.

Yet there are gaps and regions of disintegration in the poem.

Certain of the metaphors protrude with more violence than even the subject of the poem justifies. The word "fell" for all its aptness is one of these. It halts the thought and stands out like a nail that has not been pounded in to the head. It refuses to take a wholly functional place among the other words of the poem. "Dead letters" and "dull dough sours" are similar in effect.

On the other side, is not "alas!" in the eighth line flat for its place? And are not the third and fourth lines a little empty and colorless, and as if Hopkins were trying to lift them by alliteration for what they lacked in imaginative glow?

But especially I wonder if the subject of the poem is fitted for the Petrarchan sonnet form. The form has an intrinsic dignity which the idea of the poem has not. It was remarked by the mechanist that the form is very imperfectly fulfilled. The rhymes are weak and the verse broken up. Little remains of the intrinsic feeling of the form. It is as if Hopkins did his best to suppress its effect. In the manner of a sculptor trying to carve a bronze subject into marble, he is fighting the demands of his material. He is apparently deliberately weakening the character of the sonnet pattern by shattered meter and trite rhymes. Granted that here he manifests his sensitiveness to the form and is adroit in producing the best integration possible of this form and this subject, the question remains why he did not cast this poem in a form that would wholly amalgamate with his subject and would call for it.

Lastly, there is an ethical consideration that enters into the very potentialities of the subject. The subject is itself one of inner personal conflict spreading out into thoughts of contemporary cultural conflict between knowledge and myth. The conflict is represented either as unresolved or as a retreat into the myth. It is a poem of disintegrated personality. Whatever peace is hoped for is by denial and insulation from the world. The intrinsic weakness of the subject comes out clearly when it is compared with the tenor of Shakespeare's poem. In Shakespeare's sonnet there is almost as much suffering represented and much more objective cause for it. But there is a definite feeling that the issues are faced and seen in their proper proportions and finally lighted up through the relations of all the facts to one another. It is a poem with resiliency, vitality, and an inner movement of organic growth. It has a lifting and integrative effect upon the reader, and that is the very essence of value. In contrast, Hopkins' poem represents suffering with inadequate grasp of the facts, a fear to face them, no impulse to make order out of them, no integrative drive, but only despair, self-conflict, and confusion. The only thing that saves the subject is that it is so true of a certain state of disintegrative being. A broad enough reader can relate this fragmentary state of mind to the structure of his experience and of human experience as a whole. He can see it as a scientific fact in relation to other facts and so make an integration of it. But the subject has no intrinsic integrative drive.

This lack in the subject reflects a lack in the personality of the poet. We infer from the two poems compared that the personality of Shakespeare was much better integrated—had a wider grasp on the world, and had the materials within this grasp more organically interrelated—than the personality of Hopkins. So it comes that we might judge the poems (and this comment may be generalized to include all art criticism) in terms of their expression of personalities.[3]

[3] For a conception of art criticism as a realization of expressions of personality, see *Art Criticism Now* by Lionello Venturi (Baltimore: The Johns Hopkins Press, 1941). I would be loth to disparage this conception of criticism in any respect. I would even go so far as to say that in the *last* analysis (and this qualification is essential since it is only after all the ineffective, inarticulate, and mediocre personalities have been sifted out that a personality and its expressions become automatically a value in itself)—in the *last* analysis art criticism is a judgment of personality. In the *last* analysis, moreover, it is scarcely a matter of judgment at all, but a matter simply of perceiving

But this sort of criticism applies effectively only where the artists have great depth of character and a thorough mastery of their artistic techniques. It applies, in short, only to the greater artists, not to the mediocre exponents of schools who have no individuality, nor to students who have not mastered their techniques. But where it does apply, it offers a most illuminating and precise judgment. It is the judgment of character or individuality, and on the organistic view the degree of character or individuality a man has is the value of the man. It is precisely the range of this man's experience and the manner in which he has integrated it. No two great characters are alike. The greater they are the more they differentiate. Only mediocrities closely resemble each other.

In the present instance, the judgment of the value of Hopkins' poem as an expression of this poet's personality is most illuminating. He has unquestionable mastery of technique. He is no mediocrity. But he has a disintegrated character. He has perception, great range of experience, emotional sensitivity and intensity, but much disorganized.

In short, the poem has character and so is not commonplace or negligible, but it is an expression of disintegrated character. This comes out not only in the subject but in the development of the details where there is much vivid insight and much skillful organization but broken into again and again by exaggeration, deficiency, and open conflict among the demands of the aesthetic materials.

(4) *Judgment of the Formist:* We can reach the formist's judgment very quickly in the light of the previous analyses.

First, does the poem express its culture? Not typically. It

---

and understanding and having communion with these great personalities—with Spenser and Shakespeare and Milton and Dryden and Coleridge and Keats and Whitman. There is a sort of inappropriateness in comparing the greatness of great personalities, because the personality of each is so large and so unique an integration of experience, so completely individual. In the ultimate hall of fame all comparisons are invidious.

is too eccentric in technique to represent the aesthetic ideals
of nineteenth-century England, too absorbed in medieval
creed to represent the social and intellectual ideals.

Second, is it a good piece of craftsmanship and does it fulfill its genre of the sonnet form? We have already seen, not
satisfactorily. In many parts Hopkins exhibits exceptional
mastery of the poet's craft and then in other parts he is
perverse. The sonnet form, we saw, was inappropriate to the
subject, and faultily exemplified.

Third, as to whether the poem offers a representation of
the normal, or ideal and healthy man, our answer is promptly
negative. The poem is neurotic in subject and expression.
There is no relieving sense of catharsis. It is a vivid description
of a diseased mind.

In sum, there is little to be said for the poem and much to
disapprove. The main thought it leaves behind is what a pity
such poetic capacity should go to such poor purpose. But
even this thought leads to a feeling of disgust at Hopkins'
loading so deformed a human expression with such ornaments
of refined craftsmanship.

We may now collect the judgments of the poems. But it is
hardly necessary. Every judgment of Shakespeare's sonnet is
superlative. Only on the contextualistic view is Hopkins'
poem superlative. On the basis of these judgments (and clearly
they could be carried much further if there were reason to
think the features we selected for notice were unrepresentative
of the total character of either poem) it is safe to say that
Shakespeare's sonnet is a poem of exceptional beauty, and that
Hopkins' sonnet is one containing much beauty of a sort but
marred by much ugliness so that its aesthetic value is far below that of Shakespeare's poem.

Incidentally, here we may note the aesthetic utility of the
classics and of those touchstones of beauty which Matthew

Arnold made so much of. They give us concrete standards of aesthetic value by which we can gauge comparatively the concrete aesthetic value of other works. There is no sensible way of grading the beauty of Hopkins' sonnet in numerical units (and our previous analysis has shown at least one good reason why—shown that the basic aesthetic criteria are incomparable and so cannot with our present knowledge be consistently combined), but it is sensible after our study to say that Hopkins' sonnet is far inferior to Shakespeare's, and that Shakespeare's sonnet is an ideal instance of beauty.

Now it must not, of course, be thought that the value of a poem is a matter of the number of votes it gets from the different aesthetic approaches. We have gone through the process of judging these poems view by view in a mechanical way so as to bring out the sources of judgment in the clearest manner possible. And if there is doubt about the value of a work of art, recourse to this mechanical way of passing the work through these major criteria of judgment is perhaps to be recommended. But a practical critic, with the breadth of view to include all these criteria, will hold them all together in his mind and direct them upon the work abreast. There is necessarily much overlapping and repetition of judgment in the serial manner in which we have used the criteria. What alone is essential is that all of them shall be brought to bear on a work to obtain the fair and balanced judgment of it.

I wish especially for it to be noted that the different points of view are not necessarily divergent in their practical judgment of a work. All four views were in agreement in their judgment of Shakespeare's poem though often for different reasons. In the judgment of Hopkins' poem, two were in agreement and strongly negative, and two were positive, one moderately so, and the other enthusiastically so. A critic cannot say ahead how the views will combine or diverge in judgment on a specific work. In short, these philosophical views really do draw the aesthetic values out of the works of art and into the open. When they are employed as instruments of criticism their irreconcilable categorial differences in no way interfere with their coming to agreements about the values of objects. When they disagree about the values, something very significant about the object valued comes to light.

Finally, I do not wish to leave any impression that the judgments I myself have elicited from the four views in their application to these two poems are not subject to much discussion and to revision. Many things I perceived and felt in both poems I did not comment on, things I thought would not materially affect the judgment reached. I am sure I have also missed many things, and some of these might have an important bearing on the judgments. Some of my discriminations may be controversial; but I believe I have shown the manner by which aesthetic judgments can be reached and can approach a rather high degree of objectivity of a sort. It is one of the theses of these lectures that aesthetic judgment is a judgment based on facts, and is accordingly always open to new evidence and to improvement in the light of the evidence.

Here these lectures come to a close. But I promised earlier that when we had completed our study of the four relatively adequate definitions of the aesthetic field with their relevant standards, I should gather them all together into an eclectic definition, which would have a certain significance as a sort of balanced superficial summary of our present knowledge of aesthetic value. We should only be careful not to overlook the implicit conflicts lying hidden in such a composite expression.

I am sure any of you who have listened to these lectures could now easily frame such a definition. All we need to do is to take as a base one of the four definitional criteria we have studied, and qualify it by the remaining three, thus: *An ex-*

perience of beauty is one vivid in quality, highly organized, and a source of immediate enjoyment for a normal mind, or *An object of beauty is a normal perceptual integration of feelings highly pleasant, and vivid in quality.*

Such composite definitions have, I think you will agree, more appeal than the pure consistent ones we successively worked through. Eclectic definitions should have more appeal, for they encompass the factual material more completely. As between one of these eclectic definitions and *only* one of the pure consistent ones, I should choose the eclectic. But that choice is not forced upon us. We do not have to be muddled to possess the fullest wisdom. By the method we have followed (taking each point of view in turn and accepting the completely worked out judgments as a group) we can have both rational clarity in criticism and the reasonableness of wisdom.

SUPPLEMENTARY ESSAY
The Aesthetic Work of Art

THE MAIN CONCERN of aesthetic criticism is with works of art. Objects of nature—shells, ferns, mosses, trees, insects, animals, snowflakes, rock formations, mountains, water, clouds, the sun, and the moon—come in for aesthetic approval and delight, and the aesthetic perception of them is essentially the same as that for works of art, but not being objects of human construction they have not so urgently called for human criticism. Also, beyond natural objects there is a large field of experience generally regarded as aesthetic in character which we scarcely ever subject to critical judgment and usually think it rather pointless to try to criticize. I refer to dreams, reveries, objectless moods and emotions, floating images, personal thoughts, and personal activities like walking and leaping, and many types of social activity like companionship, conversation, games, business competition, intellectual argument, mutual coöperation, or the mere exhilaration of being in a crowd. All these probably fall within the aesthetic field, yet they rarely raise serious controversies of aesthetic judgment. Perhaps they should, but in fact they rarely do. The great controversies of aesthetic judgment rotate about works of art. The practical field of aesthetic criticism is thus smaller than the total aesthetic field. It is the field of works of art.

The instinct of writers on criticism to seek the justification of aesthetic criticism among the properties of the total aesthetic field is sound. But these men have tended to leap too far too soon. There has been a strange neglect of the nature of the work of art. This subject is so important that I thought an amplification of the brief analysis given in the lecture on Contextualistic Criticism might not be unwelcome. The preceding lectures, too, it seems, have been caught in this trend of the tradition in criticism, and have leaped rather far rather soon. At the risk of some repetition, I should like to offer here an analysis of the nature of the aesthetic work of art, starting from the very beginning and carrying it well beyond the sketch presented in the lectures.

What are the general characteristics of an aesthetic work of art? It is a very peculiar sort of object. In order to keep our description clear, I shall begin with just one kind of work of art, the simplest kind to describe, the one employed in the lectures, namely a picture, and then I will proceed to other kinds gathering up the various characteristics of the aesthetic work of art in general as we go along. I begin then with a description of what a picture is as a work of art. We shall take this as a sort of normal description and then later show how this norm is added to or modified in terms of other kinds of works of art. Finally we shall gather all the material together for a total rounded description. We shall find that quite a number of muddles connected with aesthetic criticism solve themselves as a result of this analysis.

To be specific, let us take as our picture the El Greco "Toledo." Now what is the aesthetic object here which is the focus of aesthetic judgment and criticism? There is the physical canvas and pigment, which El Greco worked upon, which has passed through various hands, and which now hangs on a wall of the New York Metropolitan Art Museum. There is next the subject who comes in and looks at it—you or me. Lastly there is the perception of the picture that comes to the subject whenever he looks at it. Now let us make the diagram of these three factors:

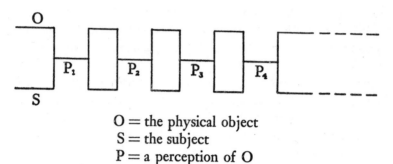

O = the physical object
S = the subject
P = a perception of O

O represents the continuity of the physical object: in our present example, the canvas and pigment of El Greco's picture. That physical picture continues right along on the wall whether perceived or not. It is represented by the continuous upper line that periodically drops into perception and out of it. When not perceived it is just O, but when perceived it is P_1, P_2, P_3, P_4, four successive perceptions into which it enters. Time is conceived as moving from left to right. Since the physical object continues in and out of perceptions, we may call it a physical continuant.

S in the diagram represents the subject such as you or me. The subject also is a continuant and exists during periods when it is not perceiving things. The subject, so far as we identify it with our physical body, is much like the physical continuant. It has mass and electrical and chemical properties, but besides these the subject has other continuous characteristics which we lump together in the term "mind." The subject has feelings, memories, thoughts, and so on, which continue when he is not perceiving. The continuity of the subject is accordingly represented in our diagram by the continuous lower line which comes up every now and then to the perception of the picture. Without committing ourselves as to whether the subject is mainly mind or body, or even upon the final validity of this distinction, we may safely for the purposes of this analysis call the subject a psychophysical continuant. In some sense, you or I or any critic continues to exist before, through, and after our perceptions of a picture.

Now, a perception occurs only when a subject and an object get into some sort of touch with each other. This contact in perception between S and O we represent by P, and the successive P_1, P_2, P_3, P_4 represent different perceptions of the same object by the same subject.

Though the diagram represents the perception as a complete merging of subject and object, that is never literally the case. Both are very complex and only parts of each actually get in touch with each other either directly or indirectly in any given perception. The physical picture has many properties that do not enter into any perception of it, and the subject (you or me) has large portions of his personality that are not touched in the perception of the picture. But not to complicate a sufficiently complicated situation even at its simplest, the diagram merely represents that in some sense in perception a physical object does get in touch with a subject like you or me, and that reciprocally you or I do get in touch with a physical object. We see the picture, and what we see is the result of ourselves and the physical picture somehow getting together. So, the diagram represents the two continuants as coming together in perception.

El Greco's physical picture O, then, hangs in a room of the museum. You or I enter the room and see it for the first time, P_1. We go out and come back and see it again, P_2, and a third time, P_3, and a fourth, P_4. The intervals between perception may be minutes, days, or years. But we go on as psychophysical continuants and the picture goes on as a physical continuant through the interims.

The repeatedly perceived picture, however, it should be noticed, is not a continuant. The perceived picture consists of a succession of intermittent perceptions—at least so far as we gather from any ordinary direct evidence concerning the situation. And what is particularly striking about this situation is that it is the *perceived picture*, not the continuous physical picture nor the continuous self who looks at it, that is the object appreciated and, if so be, critically judged. The central aesthetic object turns out to be an intermittent object made up of fugitive successive perceptions.

There are two important things to notice at once about this perceived aesthetic object—El Greco's "Toledo," for instance, as something seen. First, the features of this object— the colors and lines and volumes and movements in pictorial space and the representations of hills, buildings, and clouds —are contributed to the perception from the *two* continuants. That is what makes it legitimate to merge the two continuants in the diagram wherever a perception is indicated. The shapes, for instance, are determined partly, as we learn from physics, by the distribution of pigments on the canvas and the con- figurations of reflected light from these pigments, but partly also, as we learn from physiology and psychology, by the structure of eye and nervous system and the activities of memory, association, feeling and the like which come out of ourselves.

Just how much is contributed by the physical continuant and how much by the perceiving self in an act of perception like this is one of the much discussed problems in modern psychology and philosophy. There are a number of reputable theories of perception, some placing most of the contributions to perception in the physical continuant and leaving to the perceiving self little besides a selective activity. For such a view, the colors and the sensuous shapes and perhaps even the representations of hills and houses all lie in the physical picture, and the mind merely selects what it sees in any single act of perception. It rarely sees all that is there, and may dis- tort some features, but it makes no positive contributions to the perception. An opposite theory places nearly all of the contributions to perception in the mind of the continuant self. For this view, the colors and the sensuous shapes and the representations are all in the perceiver's mind, and the only contribution from the physical object is a stimulation of the sensory apparatus of the nervous system. All the rest is done in the mind of the perceiving self. Between these two extreme views various proportionings of the contributions are possible. But all views agree that in perception there are contributions from both the structure of the physical object and of the perceiving self, even if only a push-button stimulation from the object, or only a selective activity from the subject.

It follows that the object of aesthetic appreciation and the object of a critic's judgment in any such perception is necessarily a fugitive and intermittent object. This object occurs only when a self is actually in perceptive contact with a physical object, and lasts only as long as that contact lasts. Clear as this fact appears upon reflection, it is rarely fully taken in by writers on criticism and appreciation. The preponderant tendency is to identify the aesthetic object either with some conception of a physical continuant, or with some completely mental activity.

Since the aesthetic object in the appreciation and judgment of a work of art is always a perceived object, it is clear that here at least such identifications as those just mentioned cannot be made. For the one characteristic that makes a perception a perception and not an image or a dream is that some contribution enters into the situation from both sides. How to proportion these contributions in detail need not concern us at this stage. The important thing is to see that in the normal act of critical aesthetic judgment we are dealing with perceptions, and that perceptions in their very nature are fugitive and depend on some degree of temporary co-operation between a physical object and a self. It will be best if we assume for the present that there is a rather large contribution from both sides.

So far, then, we have discovered that the object of critical aesthetic judgment is perceptions which are the fugitive and intermittent results of contributions from two continuants. The next thing we discover is that the successive perceptions (P_1, P_2, P_3, P_4), which a single subject has of a single physical object, carry a cumulative effect. The first time we look at the El Greco, for instance, we may notice principally the threatening clouds and the hills; the next time the dynamic movement of the forms; the next time details here and there that we had not noticed like the little figures down in the stream; the next time subtle repetitions of shapes; and so on. All of these perceptions are ordinarily regarded as relevant to the aesthetic object, and in giving a critical judgment of it are considered features to be taken account of. There are, moreover, certain psychological mechanisms that make it possible to carry over the results of one perception to considerable degree into the next, so that successive perceptions tend to become enriched by those that have gone before. This action is sometimes called "funding." A late perception in a series thus carries to considerable degree the results of previous perceptions as its constituents.

The cumulative effect is thus of two sorts. In part, it consists in finding more and more in the object, adding detail to detail out of the physical object through the successive perceptions. So far as this effect goes, each new perception might be quite different from its predecessor, since it brings out something quite new in the object. The only unity in the perceptive series so viewed would be the fact that the perceptions were all stimulated by the same physical continuant. The unity of the successive perceptions of a single object is, however, clearly much greater than that. This is achieved by the second sort of cumulative effect which we called funding.

Through funding previous perceptions are carried over into later ones by of memory and recognition, so that a later perception in some degree summarizes all its predecessors.

The object of aesthetic judgment and of appreciation in a work of art, then, is not this, that, or the other perception as it comes, but rather the total series, P_1-P_2-P_3-P_4, which we shall call the *perceptive series*. This is literally the aesthetic work of art. Different aesthetic philosophies differ in their ways of handling and interpreting this series. But in some sense or other it is clear that this perceptive series is the aesthetic object in the critical judgment and appreciation of works of art. The actual aesthetic object for the practical critic or everyday spectator is not a physical object, nor an idea, nor even a single act of perception, but the intermittent cumulative succession of perceptions which we call the perceptive series.

The peculiarities of aesthetic judgment, and the uncertainty on the part of many critics as to just what it is they are judging, all derive from the peculiarity of this practical object of aesthetic criticism and appreciation, for it is not a continuous object but an intermittent object, and it is not a succession of identically repeated perceptions but is a succession of perceptions with a cumulative growth at least up to a point.

Light begins to dawn on the problem of criticism when the situation is fully realized in this sense, and fully accepted. There is a strong tendency among critics and writers on aesthetics to try to reduce the aesthetic object to one of the continuants which make it up, or else to try to break it down into the atomic perceptions or transitory states that are cumulatively collected into its totality. These attempts to simplify the problem miss it at the start. We shall have many qualifications and amplifications to make of this primary analysis of a work of art. But the original facts from which any constructive thought about aesthetic criticism must clearly start are those which we have just elicited and have represented in our diagram. We may summarize them as follows:

A. In practical criticism, a critic is dealing with perceptions.

B. The content of these perceptions is partly a contribution from a continuous physical object, partly a contribution from a continuous psychophysical subject.

C. The aesthetic work of art and object of criticism is not a continuant, but an intermittent series of perceptions with a cumulative effect, namely, the perceptive series.

The analysis so far has been frankly preliminary and tentative. The illustration held in mind was of only one kind of work of art, a painting; and we took into consideration only one perceiver. We must now spread our analysis over the great variety of works of art that there are, and over the great variety of subjects perceiving them. We must consider variations in the physical continuants and in the psychophysical continuants. And first we ask, what variations are there in the physical continuants?

We shall pass under review the principal kinds of works of art. These kinds are associated with what are called "arts." All sorts of theoretical classifications of the arts can be made, but the classification that holds in practice, and so may be called the actual classification (the common division into painting, sculpture, architecture, music, literature, drama, and dance), is based on the nature of the physical continuants and on the limits of human capacities in dealing with them. It is physical materials together with the techniques for handling them that separate the aesthetic arts from one another.

If we may make a distinction between the ground for division and the reason for it, we may say that the *ground* for the actual divisions among the arts lies in the diverse materials out of which physical works of art are made, but that the *reason* lies in the limited technical capacities of men. Physical materials demand special techniques to handle them. It ordinarily takes all of a man's time to master one major technique. Few men become expert at more than one. For that reason the men training in one technique inevitably gather together in schools, and tend to continue together ever after, for, in a sense, the schooling never ceases. The divisions among the arts are thus divisions among men who from the limitations of human powers have had to become specialists in creative techniques, which techniques in turn depend upon the physical materials of the work of art.[1]

Accordingly, in comparing the characteristic features of works from the various arts, we may expect to find a good many striking differences. But, at the same time, we shall discover some surprising hidden similarities. For we shall find that prominent features of works of art in one art were present but overlooked in the works of another art. By these comparisons we can thus gain a much more complete understanding of what a work of art as an object of critical and appreciative judgment is.

So far we have been dealing only with a painting. A painting, however, presents the simplest problem for the kind of

---

[1] This empirical analysis of the grounds for the classification of the arts exposes the fallacy of theories of criticism based on the criterion of the "purity of the arts," the criterion by which mixed or "mongrel" arts are disparaged. As a matter of fact, the technique of any major art is already a mixture of many minor techniques. On the "purity of art" criterion a painting in color would be a mongrel, since it mixes the technique of form with that of color. The El Greco would be an egregious mongrel, since it mixes not only form and color techniques but a variety of techniques of representation in light and shade, perspective, etc. A symphony would be something below contempt, since it combines the arts of twenty odd instruments. Any theater art would rate still lower, since theater is in the person of a director precisely a special technique of mingling techniques. And the opera—well, the criterion of purity was particularly designed to dispose of the opera! Of course, some modes of mixing techniques do not work. But there is no evidence for any intrinsic perfection in the virginity of an art.

analysis we have been doing. (Do not think this means that pictures are easier to criticize than other works of art. If anything, the contrary. I only mean that the analysis of the main factors involved in a work of art is most easily brought out in the case of a picture.) For in a picture we are concerned with only one physical object, and with only one surface of that object, and with that total surface open to vision whenever the picture is an object of appreciation. Moreover, the medium of light that reflects to the eye the patterns of pigments on the canvas is so transparent as to be easily overlooked and nearly negligible. The perceiver seems to be in direct touch with the controlling physical continuant, so that the merging of this physical continuant literally with the subject in perception (as shown in the diagram) closely describes the appearance of the situation.

Now, when we turn to sculpture, the situation is immediately complicated by the relevant use of the three dimensions. A statue in the round has a multiplicity of aspects or points of view, where a picture has but one.

There is still ordinarily just one statue standing as the work of art, say Michelangelo's "Moses." There is only one original "Moses." But a single adequate view of the "Moses" means walking all around it and synthesizing the perceptions of each aspect into a connecting circuit of aspects. The single visual statue is the whole circuit of aspects. The perceptual judgment involved in building up this aesthetic object thus requires a synthesis of juxtaposed aspects which is not involved in the appreciation of a picture. In the appreciation of a statue, one complete grasp of it, so to speak, requires a synthesis of a succession of perceptual aspects. A picture has only one aspect. Every aspect of a statue, of course, carries its own perceptive series. We thus learn the distinction between a perceptive series and a perceptual grasp, which is a summation and synthesis of the perceptive series of all the relevant aspects of the physical continuant. We see that a picture is a special case in which the perceptual grasp is telescoped into a single aspect. Most works of art have many aspects and demand the extension of the perceptive series, which we described in terms of one aspect only, to every aspect of the perceptual grasp. We may imagine a methodical subject who looks at a statue several times and each time makes a complete circuit of its aspects. With each circuit we then complete one perceptual grasp. But with each circuit he is also building up his perceptive series for each aspect. The total result would then have to be symbolized somewhat like the following, supposing that we considered four aspects: P^A, being a perception of aspect A, P^B of aspect B, P^C of C, and P^D of D. And G will stand for a perceptual grasp as a result of a circuit of the aspects.

$$G_1(P^{A_1} + P^{B_1} + P^{C_1} + P^{D_1}) + G_2(P^{A_2} + P^{B_2} + P^{B_3} + P^{B_4}) +$$
$$G_3(P^{C_1} + P^{C_2} + P^{C_3} + P^{C_4}) + G_4(P^{D_1} + P^{D_2} + P^{D_3} + P^{D_4})$$

It is clear that this is just a complication of our original perceptive series to take care of a variety of aspects when, as usually, these occur. An aesthetic work of art in sculpture is made up of perceptions in intermittent cumulative series just as in painting, but the organization of these perceptions is more complex due to the presence of diverse aspects.

Of course, actually an appreciative critic does not build up his aesthetic statue in the methodical way diagrammed but in a much more haphazard (or rather sensitively controlled) manner. A man does not always take in every aspect of a statue each time he looks at it. He builds up his perceptual grasp of it simultaneously with his enrichment of the different aspects, and usually some aspects are intrinsically richer than others and require much more funding.

In architecture even more than in sculpture we see the importance of the perceptual grasp. For a building is not only three dimensional but has an inside relevant to aesthetic perception as well as an outside. Moreover, the aspects of a building are not all visual. There are many tactile and kinaesthetic aspects having to do with the texture of materials which are intended to be felt, walked upon, sat upon, and the like, and there are spaces to be walked through, and to, and from. Some of these, we notice, sculpture also often has. It should not, however, be assumed that differences of sensory material in perception involve differences of aspect, as if tactile sensations could not merge with visual. Besides, the further one goes in building up the perceptive materials of a work of art the harder it becomes to decide whether we are repeating perceptions of a single aspect or getting a new perceptive aspect and the more arbitrary the distinction seems. The essential thing is to be well aware of the different sorts of perceptive materials in a work of art to see that we miss none. But in a broad way, the distinction between an intensive appreciation of one aspect through a perceptive series and an organization of a number of aspects through a perceptual grasp is a useful one.

Turning from the visual arts to music we come upon a number of new features that still further add to our understanding of the nature of a work of art. In music the physical continuant is the musical score. And this is a set of symbols on paper.

The audible structure perceived by the senses is sounds produced by musical instruments or the human voice. Musical instruments are, of course, also physical continuants as well as the performers who convert the symbols of the score into the patterns of sounds perceived; but the perceived patterns of sounds are preserved not in the instruments but in the score. The instruments and those who perform upon them are in the nature of a medium between the physical continuant and the perceiving subject. And in this instance the medium is alone what is prominent in direct perception, while the score which determines the structure of the perception is pushed out of sight of the perceiver and is in the nature of a remote control. Literally one does not perceive the score in musical appreciation; one perceives the sound patterns controlled by the score. Yet the sound patterns literally perceived have no permanence apart from the score as a physical continuant. The score in practical criticism is as essential to a rich cumulative aesthetic judgment of a work of music as the canvas and pigments of a painting or the marble and bronze of a statue. Clearly the patterns symbolized in the score do pass over into the auditory perception as a definite contribution from the physical continuant. What strikes us in the physical setup for music is the very important function a medium may have on the physical side of the perceptive situation. Actually in every perception except a purely tactile one a medium is involved, and the physical continuant is more or less remote from the subject. Every visual work of art, for instance, depends upon the medium of light. In music the controlling continuant is simply more remote than usual, and its contribution to perception more indirect. The contribution from the score, however, is definitely contained in the auditory perception, just as much as if it were directly given off the mediating instruments—as in graphophone records it actually is. The remoteness of the physical continuant in music, or wherever it occurs, does not, therefore, make any serious modification in our original analysis.

It does, however, frequently result in a splitting of the judgment in an aesthetic work of art. There will be a judgment on the continuant and a judgment on the medium. So, critics will make certain judgments of a composer's composition and other judgments on the performer's interpretation. We tend to take it for granted that the judgment of the composition is really of the score or physical continuant with

an assumption of perfect performance, and that the judgment
of the performer's interpretation is about the medium. However, when the medium is human as the performer of a musical
instrument is, the judgment about the medium may become
very important, even exceeding in interest that of the continuant. Scores may then be written mainly as instruments to
exhibit the performers. Then the situation becomes almost
reversed, the score becoming practically a medium for a voice
or a technique, and the voice or technique in the body of the
performer becoming the physical continuant. This rivalry
for the center of judgment is always possible where the
medium is human, and it is one of the problems of criticism to
distribute the judgments properly for any particular work of
art, and also to consider the degree of aesthetic justification
for that particular distribution. It is fairly safe to say that the
greater the aesthetic value of the composition or score in its
own right the greater the aesthetic necessity for a performer
to regard himself as only a medium to convert the symbols of
the score into the perceptual materials they signify. There are
no scores, however, that do not admit of some freedom of
interpretation on the part of the performer, so that the
nature of a performance calls for criticism as well as the
composition. Whenever a work of art passes through the
medium of a human interpreter it is safe to say that a twofold judgment is always required, one on the contribution
from the continuant, and one on that from the interpreter.
Both belong intrinsically to such an aesthetic work of art,
for the work must be interpreted in some way to become
perceptible. From this observation we discover that a single
work of art may have several valid alternative interpretations,
all belonging equally to it. The complete judgment of the
total work would thus have to consider all the valid interpretations.

Once we get this idea, we realize that in some degree any

kind of work of art may have alternative interpretations. In a painting, for instance, lines may now be taken as representative symbols, and now as abstract plastic elements. The painting may be perceived exclusively as a representation, or exclusively as a plastic structure. These two interpretations can indeed be combined in one that includes both. But also identical lines may function now as depth cues with one set of forms in the picture, and now with another set of forms as a surface arabesque, and these latter two interpretations are contrary to each other and cannot be combined in a single clear perception, any more than two musical interpretations can—though each may carry the funded memory of the other in its outskirts.

So, we learn that in the perceptive structure of a work of art there may be intrinsic ambiguities, alternative interpretations. According to some views, the greater the quantity of these ambiguities the richer the work, and the greater its aesthetic value. Here, accordingly, is one respect in which an aesthetic object differs markedly from a scientific object since the latter is expected to be unequivocal. And here again we receive a warning against trying to impose scientific and practical criteria of objectivity upon the aesthetic object. The criteria of objectivity in the two fields are quite different.

But besides bringing out the possible remoteness of control of a physical continuant, and the possibility of alternative interpretations relevant to a physical continuant, a musical score reveals another peculiarity of many works of art. For a musical score is what may be called a multiple physical continuant. There are hundreds of scores of any well-known piece of music. Whereas there is only one genuine El Greco "Toledo," there are thousands of scores of Beethoven's Fifth Symphony, any one of them as genuine a physical continuant as another. We need not dilate upon this feature because it is so obvious. It conduces greatly, incidentally, to the preservation of a work of art. A multiple continuant is much harder to destroy than a single continuant, though one be made of paper and the other of stone.

And again once we get the idea of a work of art being a multiple continuant on its physical side, we see that many kinds of works of art are so constituted. There are often several genuine copies of a bronze statue. Prints, such as woodblocks, lithographs, etchings, have multiple continuants. Most ceramics and textiles have multiple continuants.

While we are on this topic we should note the assistance that can be given in building up our perceptive structure of a work of art by reproductions of various sorts. There is, for instance, a good reproduction of El Greco's "Toledo." The reproduction is a multiple continuant with a great deal of merit of its own. But this merit is all derived from its approximation to the genuine El Greco. Many people who speak of the "Toledo" have never seen anything but the reproduction. And to a certain approximation they have actually perceptive material relevant to the original picture. Perhaps we should admit the conception of approximate multiple continuants, such as reproductions of all kinds (including graphophone records and the like in music, and translations in literature), and note that these may add perceptive material that is literally incorporated into the aesthetic structure of the genuine work of art. They are in a shadowy way part of the physical continuant of the work of art.

One more feature comes to us with a degree of novelty out of an examination of the functioning of the musical work of art, and that is the nature of its perceptual grasp. A musical composition resembles a statue or a building in requiring a perceptual grasp. But the temporal perceptual grasp of a piece of music is different from the spatial perceptual grasp of a visual object. A statue may be walked around in either direction. The various exterior and interior aspects of a building may be gathered from many routes. But the diverse auditory perceptions that go to make up one hearing or perceptual grasp of a musical composition are meant to be passed through by one route only. A musical composition is, of course, a multitude of diverse perceptions, for the duration of a single present perception cannot exceed a few moments. When we are hearing the second phrase of a piece of music, the first phrase has passed into memory and is no longer directly heard. The total hearing of a musical composition is a succession of such auditory perceptions overlapping one another. These are synthesized in the perceptual grasp of the whole piece. And in a piece of music this synthesis is intended to be made in one direction only, passing from the beginning to the end. A section of a piece of music may be taken out and quoted, but, for just criticism and appreciation, it must be felt in its place in the total sequence as so far from the beginning with such and such musical material to follow. The direction and route of the perceptual grasp are rigidly fixed in music.

Once we observe this demand strongly working in music, we may look back and see it also working less prominently in the visual arts. Aspects must be seen in their place in the total space organization, too, and within limits are intended to be approached in certain ways. A building is generally constructed with definite approaches, and visual climaxes are composed in view of these approaches. But a spatial work of art is not subject to the single rigorous order of time, in the way a temporal work of art is. In short, there is a freedom of routes for a perceptual grasp in most visual works of art, but only one route in a temporal work of art.

When we turn to works of literature we meet some new surprises. Here the strictly sensuous perceptual factor seems to drop out altogether. The physical continuant is the printed book or poem. This like the musical score is a set of symbols, and like the musical score there are hundreds of copies of the book all of them equally good substitutes for one another. A book is a multiple continuant. Moreover a work of literature like a piece of music is a temporal work of art and demands a perceptual grasp along one route only. One reading of a book or poem is like one hearing of a piece of music.

But, different from music, a book or poem is ordinarily read directly off the printed page by the person appreciating it. The physical continuant is not a remote control of the aesthetic work of art in literature, but the direct stimulus. It is, most amazingly, the intervening physical stimuli of perception, such as the sounds of music that are wanting. In the ordinary experience of reading a book a sensuous content is almost totally lacking and in its place are images and meanings all aroused entirely within the mind of the reader, as we say. Strictly speaking there is practically no perception at all. In terms of our original analysis of the diagram, this is amazing.

It might be said that the act of reading a book or poem to oneself is a telescoped act in which a literal perception of a narrator's or a bard's voice is understood. That is, it could be argued that the prototype or norm of reading and appreciating a literary work of art is reading it aloud, so that the sounds and rhythms of the words are perceptually heard just as in music. It could be pointed out that even music can be read off the score by a highly trained musician and heard and appreciated in his mind, without the actual intervening perception of the audible tones produced on musical instruments. But a musician never (or, at least, very rarely) regards this sort of appreciation as an adequate substitute for the actually perceived sounds. He reads music from the score only when it is inconvenient to produce it on an instrument, and he likes to verify his mental appreciation with an actual perceptual one.

To a certain degree this may be said to be true of poetry where the sounds of the words and their rhythms count heavily in the appreciation of the aesthetic work of art. We are often told that we should read a poem aloud if we want to appreciate it fully. We probably always should. But actually we rarely do. We feel so sure of the reliability of our images of the sounds and rhythms that we regard the sensations of them unnecessary. When it comes to prose, however, in reading novels and essays where much less weight is ordinarily thrown upon the sounds of the words, then it seems rather ridiculous to ask us to read aloud. Certainly these works are rarely, if ever, written with this expectation. We must, I think, accept the situation that at least for a large portion of literature an actual perception of the sounds of the words is not expected but only an adequate image of them. A work of literature is not, it would seem, exactly analogous to a piece of music. No rich sensuous perception is regularly expected between the symbols of a page and the experienced aesthetic content. The pages of a book are as a rule not a remote control as in music, but the direct control of the aesthetic work of art. In this respect the physical continuant in literature resembles that of a visual work of art. It is, in fact, a visual stimulus. But it differs from a picture or statue in being almost entirely symbolic, and in this respect resembles, as we said, a musical score.

An important qualification of our original analysis is obviously called for to take care of the non-perceptual character of the typical literary work of art. There is a tendency to carry the qualification to an extreme, however. Because no perceptual material of any great importance appears in the silent reading of a book or poem, it is tempting to place the literary work of art entirely within the subject, and to deny that there is any relevant physical contribution whatever. The physical book is just a lot of symbols, it is said, black marks on a page. These do not literally enter into the immediate content of the appreciated poem nor novel, which is entirely produced out of the mental activities of the subject. The subject, it is tempting to say, contributes everything to the aesthetic work of art, and the physical printed book nothing. But this is clearly false, since were it not for the printed book there would be no more communicable form in literature than in idle revery.

We have here a type of experience that has received no name. For it is not strictly imagining or thinking since these experiences are supposed to go on without external control. And the term perception is usually regarded as involving sensory material, which, as we have shown, is very nearly lacking from this sort of experience. This sort of experience is that of externally controlled imagery and thought. I propose to call it "unsensory perception."

And as with the other observations we have made with different sorts of works of art so here once we notice the fact of perceptual control of other than sensory material, we are aware that in varying degrees this goes on in every work of art. Every sort of work of art wakes and controls images, thoughts, and, while we are about it, emotions and memories as well. There is no set limit to the material which may enter into a perception. In fact, if there were only sensory material in a perception we should find that the experience was merely sensation, a mere aggregate of sensations. It is the seepage of meanings and memories into the sensation aggregate that coagulates the whole into what is properly called a perception. El Greco's "Toledo" is full of meanings and recognitions and so is Beethoven's Fifth Symphony. But ordinarily in perception there is a firm relevant core of sensation in which these meanings inhere. In literature this relevant sensory core is omitted. The whole perception is essentially unsensory.

Literature serves also to bring out another feature, and one, moreover, which our original diagram did not at all represent. That is the cultural contribution. Every work of art contains a cultural contribution, and it is often very hard to discern just how great this is. But in a work of literature it is easy to see that at least all that it owes to language is a cultural contribution. A language exists in some sense outside the physical continuant and outside the subject. The meanings of words—all that is connoted by the term "usage"—are not derived from the purely personal reactions of the subject and are certainly not contained in the physical ink stimuli on a page. The subject and the stimuli are the channels through which the cultural contribution finds its way into the aesthetic work of art, but these channels are not the source of the contribution. This point is not brought out in our original simple analysis and must be recognized.

Culture means a system of social relationships; and cultural objects are the instruments that mediate these relationships. Some writers on art tend to absorb all of art into culture and to treat works of art as if they were nothing but cultural objects. For them criticism resolves itself into an analysis of the social relationships exhibited in art, descriptions of schools and styles of art tracing the sources and development of these, examinations of the influence of religion, economic, political, and other institutions upon art, comparisons of cultural institutions to mark general cultural traits that run through a period and characterize the whole art of a period. Art is thus regarded as a cultural institution, and works of art as expressions of the culture of a period. Any single work of art is an item in this cultural expression.

In this way of treating a work of art its aesthetic value, the sort of thing we have been describing in the lectures, tends to be either neglected or to be equated with the degree in which the work expresses or influences its culture. This cultural factor in aesthetic criticism has been repeatedly recognized in the lectures, particularly in the formistic account. But from our point of view, and on the basis of our previous analyses, the proposal to absorb all aesthetic questions in cultural questions is clearly an attempt to reduce a work of art to one of its factors only.

There is also a contrary danger of neglecting the cultural factor and trying to reduce it to physical and psychophysical terms. With one's attention on the perception of a single work of art, it is easy to forget the cultural factor, since this enters into the perception not directly but always through the channels of the physical continuant and the subject continuant. A cultural institution is also in a sense a continuant which makes its contribution to the aesthetic work of art, but it is not clearly discernible until we are forced to consider the influence of other men upon any one man's perceptions. Language forces this consideration upon us, since verbal symbols could not control a man's meanings except through the social compulsion of usage. And once we have noticed the nature and the extent of the cultural contribution in one kind of work of art, we become aware of it in all others. Whatever acts like language in a work of art is a cultural contribution. We accordingly add culture as a third continuant that makes its contribution to the work of art.

Of the chief kinds of works of art there now remains only that of the theater. The group of theater arts have the common trait of being performed on a stage. In the drama the physical continuant is the written play, which controls the characters on the stage; and the actors and the scenery and lighting are the direct stimuli for the perceived aesthetic object. A drama, accordingly, closely resembles a piece of music. It has a remote control and the patterns of the physical continuant are transmitted to the perceiving subject through performers. In the drama, however, the performing actors are generally expected to contribute more by themselves to the perceived object than the performers of music. The *visual* characterization is almost entirely in their hands.

In the dance, however, we come again upon something new.

Here the physical continuant in the ordinary sense as a source of constant control practically disappears. This is almost as surprising as the disappearance of a sensory medium in literature. In the dance there is a good strong sensory medium in the form of our visual sensation of the dancers' bodies. But there is no physical continuant of any importance like the written play in the drama or the score in music. We do not think of choreographic charts as things to study for criticism, —as yet, at least. And a choreographer is more like a play director or orchestral conductor than like a dramatist or composer. The continuance of a dance depends upon the life of the dancer, or the holding together of a dance troupe—or on the transmission of a tradition from group to group and from generation to generation. That is why the dance is strongest in those localities where there is a strong tradition of the dance. In short, a cultural continuant takes the place of a physical continuant.

The peculiarity of the dance, then, is that, lacking an ordinary physical continuant, this is replaced by a cultural continuant, the patterns of which are transmitted to perception through the medium of the dancers. The cultural continuant thus acts as a remote control upon the perceptual structure, just like a written play or a musical score except that its locus of existence is not on physical paper but in men's memories.

Before books were written, literature, of course, also relied upon a cultural continuant in the memories of bards. The dance serves to remind us that the cultural factor may on occasion serve as a controlling continuant in place of the physical continuant. To some degree it probably functions in this way in all works of art. Wherever the perceptions of a work of art are directly controlled by tradition, there we have evidence of the action of a cultural continuant.

We have now passed in review various important types of works of art, and noticed the variations they produce upon our original simple analysis. This amounts to a more careful description of the nature of the physical continuant and its effects upon the aesthetic perception.

It remains to ask what effects upon this perception come to light when we consider the contributions of a variety of subjects. Our answer here may be quite brief because already in answering the first question we have been forced to trespass upon the second. For we have already been forced to notice the contribution of a culture, and a culture presupposes a multiplicity of subjects. Within these subjects as a group and in the texture of their mutual relations and activities, a culture has its life and its existential locus.

When we are led to consider the question of the effects of many subjects upon the aesthetic work of art, we discover that our interest shifts from trying to find how much variety is produced to trying to find how much uniformity can be asserted to exist in the object of all these subjects' perceptions. The presence of a multiplicity of subjects before a work of art suggests the possibility of a great relativity of perception. If a hundred different subjects look at El Greco's "Toledo" will there not be a hundred different subjective contributions to the perceived object, and so a hundred different perceptions, and so again a hundred different aesthetic objects? Is El Greco's "Toledo" in any legitimate sense a single aesthetic work of art to so many subjects, or is it not as numerous as the subjects that see it? We are faced again with the question of the objectivity of the work of art. How much stability, constancy, invariancy has it, if any? We have been assuming in this essay that it has much. Moreover our analysis so far must have assured us that an extreme aesthetic relativism cannot be maintained. For the physical continuant at any rate is nearly or quite changeless. Its contribution to the aesthetic object is practically constant whatever variety the subjects' contributions may produce.

But there are also two other pervasive factors making for a considerable degree of uniformity and these are on the subjects' side. They are the biological and the cultural factors. Men are all of one species, and apart from color blindness, tone deafness, and similar physiological and psychological defects can be counted on to perceive about the same thing. Where the defects exist we have means for detecting them and for judging how much men so constituted lack of the full perception of a work of art. Likewise, so far as men partake of a common culture, we can count on a constancy in the subjects' contribution.

Furthermore, it must not be forgotten that the aesthetic work of art is not realized in any casual perception but is a perceptive series and involves a perceptual grasp. Normally constituted men brought up in the same culture may approach a work of art from quite different aspects and obtain quite different initial perceptions, but as they enlarge their perceptive series and build up the total perceptive structure of the work of art, this total structure is bound to become more and more nearly identical for the various men.

Due to similar biological constitution, and a common culture when participated in, and the funding of the earlier perceptions with the later in the perceptive series, there is altogether what may be called a convergence effect towards a pretty high degree of identity in the total perceptive series of different subjects—that is, in the aesthetic work of art. The aesthetic work of art is, in fact, the common object of these subjects. It is that which the constancy of the physical continuant, the common biological constitution of the subjects, a culture common to these subjects, and the fully rounded experience which we call the total perceptive series of these subjects brings into being. All of these factors, it should be noticed, came out of our preceding analysis. We are simply putting them together and noticing the result, and the result is something with quite an impressive objectivity and constancy.

The aesthetic work of art actually involves a multiplicity of subjects, just as it involves a multiplicity of perceptions. What we have called the convergence effect here among subjects corresponds to the funding effect among perceptions. Just as the aesthetic work of art is no single perception but the result of the total perceptive series, so the aesthetic work of art is not the perception of any one subject but a convergence effect among the perceptions of many subjects, which cancels out individual idiosyncrasies. The aesthetic work of art is thus not a private object. It intrinsically involves, in the way we have shown, other subjects. Or to put it another way, we find upon complete analysis that the subject continuant of a work of art is always a multiple continuant.

Now let us gather together the traits of a work of art which we have successively discovered in the course of our analysis. A work of art involves (1) a physical continuant and (2) a subject continuant. These make contributions to perceptions, and give rise to (3) a perceptive series with a funding effect. This intermittent perceptive series is the aesthetic work of art in its barest form. Generally, however, a work of art has numerous aspects (each with its own perceptive series) which become organized through (4) a perceptual grasp. Also, the physical continuant is rarely in direct contact with the subject and exerts a (5) remote control over perception through a (6) medium. When the medium is human performers and interpreters of the remote controlling physical continuant as in music and drama, a twofold judgment is required, one on the physical continuant proper, and one on the interpretation. Several equally valid interpretations may thus be intrinsic to a work of art, and in general (7) intrinsic ambiguities are characteristic of most works of art. Many works of art have (8) multiple physical continuants. Some lack a sensory medium and are built up from (9) "unsensory perceptions," from which we note that all works of art have more or less material that is not sensory. All works of art participate in (10) cultural continuants. In some works of art there is no physical continuant and a cultural continuant takes its place. (11) The subject continuant is always a multiple continuant. There is finally (12) a convergence effect in every work of art functioning through (a) the constant physical continuant, (b) the biological uniformity of the human subjects, (c) a common culture, and (d) the funding effect in the perceptive series, all of which tend towards a considerable objectivity and stability in the perceptive structure of the aesthetic work of art.

This is the object of aesthetic criticism. The field of such objects is the field of aesthetic criticism.

There is one remaining point to bring out. This object, as we have seen, is a perceptual object. Throughout all this analysis of the aesthetic work of art not a word has been said about its value. Up to a certain level nothing needs be said. Whatever the value placed upon the object, as a perceptual object it remains unchanged. This point is particularly clear if the aesthetic judgment is given in terms of pleasure. Two men could entirely agree about a very discriminating, highly funded perception of a Botticelli or a Matisse and one would like it and another would not. The disagreement is not over the content of the perception, which is essentially the same for both spectators, but over the value found in it.

Similarly, two men could have almost exactly the same highly funded and discriminating perception of Hopkins' sonnet "I Wake, and Feel the Fell of Dark," and one judge it ugly on hedonistic grounds and the other judge it very beautiful on contextualistic grounds. In this instance, they might both agree that it was disagreeable.

There is clearly a distinction that can be made up to a certain level between a judgment of aesthetic perception and a judgment of aesthetic value. And up to this level we can expect more objectivity or ultimate agreement regarding the perceptual judgment of a work of art than regarding the judgment of its value. This point is an important one to see. For many people, especially those who identify values with pleasures, are likely to think that the objectivity of an aesthetic work of art is no greater than that of the judgment of its aesthetic value. Our analysis shows, on the contrary, that there may be wide discrepancies in the judgments of the value of an aesthetic work of art, along with close agreement as to the perceptual judgment of it.

However, our analysis also shows that this can be expected only up to a certain level. There comes a point where the value judgment has a direct effect upon the perceptual judgment. This appears most clearly in comparing an organicist's perceptions with a mechanist's. According to the latter, a definite distinction can be made between the hearing of a dissonance and the liking or disliking of it. According to the mechanist, the perceptual object heard by two equally competent critics when listening to a piece of modern music could well be practically identical, so that they could agree about the total structure of the composition to minute detail, yet one dislike it and the other like it, *because of the dissonances*. That is, the perceptual object is regarded as just the same, but one critic does not enjoy its contents and finds it ugly, while the other does enjoy its contents and finds it beautiful.

Now, according to an organicist, these two perceptions are not alike in their content. For, according to him, a well composed piece of music is an organic structure in which every detail is integrated with every other so that the character of the work of art as a complete individual organism permeates every part of it. For him, the fully funded perceptual judgment of the piece of music (supposing it to be in fact well integrated) is the perception of this harmoniously integrated whole. It follows that the critic who cannot enjoy the dissonances in their place in this musical structure, cannot even perceive the structure. His perceptual judgment is deficient, according to the organicist, because his dislike of the dissonances keeps him from integrating them into the harmonious whole which in fact is perceptually there to be heard by a competent ear. The perceptual judgment and the judgment of value at this level of criticism accordingly merge and mutually affect each other.

In the preceding lectures our discussion was largely on this rather high level. We were as much concerned over the nature of aesthetic perception as over the judgment of value. The organicist, we saw, demands an integrated perception, the formist a normal perception, the contextualist a vivid perception, the mechanist a discriminating perception. These perceptual demands do ultimately have an effect on the content of a perceptual object viewed according to these modes of interpretation. And these perceptual demands emanate from the interpretations of aesthetic value intrinsic to the respective world hypotheses. The perceptual judgment and the judgment of value do ultimately affect each other.

However, on the lower levels of criticism the perceptual judgment of an aesthetic work of art can be kept practically apart from the judgment of its aesthetic value. And it is often useful to do this. For persons who would start disagreeing at once about the aesthetic value of a work may be induced to reach a great deal of discriminating agreement about its perceptual content. Then they may be surprised in the end to find that their judgments of its value are not so divergent as they first supposed.

With due consideration of personal idiosyncrasies of inheritance, and the influences of environment and culture, there does not seem to be any insurmountable reason according to our analysis why highly objective judgments should not be obtainable not only of the aesthetic content of a work of art but also of its aesthetic value.

Index

Aesthetic attitude, 76
Aesthetic conscience, 94
Aesthetic dishonesty, 92
Aesthetic material, 79
Aesthetics, 8
  contextualistic, 56
  "from above," 24
  systematic, 48
Alexander, S., 98
Ambiguity in work of art, 157 ff.
Analysis, contextualistic, 58 ff.
Animism, 14
A priori, 8, 17, 29, 31
Aquinas, Thomas, 98
Architecture, 150, 153–154
Aristotle, 32, 97, 109, 111, 112
Arnold, Matthew, 139
Art (cf. work of art)
  classification of, 150
  criticism, 22
  and equilibrium, 111
  mongrel, 151
  purity of, 151
  representative, 116
  value in, 74
Artist, 88 ff.
  weakness of, 94
Augustine, 98
Authority, 17
  criterion of, 13, 25
  infallible, 5
Average (*vs.* normal), 102, 113

Bach, J. S., 109
Beauty (cf. value, aesthetic), 87, 92,
    96, 122, 138 ff., 141
  difficult, 93
  as exemplification of norm, 107
  theory of (cf. aesthetics), 81
Beethoven, L., 45, 109, 157

Bergson, Henri, 56
Berkeley, George, 42
Böcklin, A., 112
Botticelli, S., 169
Bosanquet, B., 75 ff.
Brancusi, C., 25
Breughel, P., 109

Calvinistic ideas, 36
Cannon, W. B., 64
Categories
  contextualistic, 58 ff.
  mechanistic, 36 ff.
  organistic, 74 ff., 92
  of world hypotheses, 22, 24, 33,
    140
Catharsis, 127, 138
  theory, 111, 112
Certainty, 5
Classics, 138
Classification of the arts, 150–151
Coleridge, S. T., 16, 59, 60, 64, 90,
    137
Common sense, 10, 22, 28, 48
  criterion, 12
  test definition, 23, 27, 32, 43–44, 56
Conflict, 65 ff., 90, 112, 122
Consciousness, 38, 40
Contextualism, 9, 20, 54 ff., 74, 97,
    171
Contextualistic aesthetic, 87, 90, 96
Contextualistic tone, 76, 77, 169
Continuant
  cultural, 164–165, 169
  multiple, 157, 160, 168
  physical (= work of art), 144 ff.,
    168
  psychophysical (= subject, spec-
    tator), 145 ff., 168–169
Convergence effect, 167–169